T0106602

BIBLE STORIES AND CONTEMPORARY TIMES IN POETIC LINES

AUGUSTINE JOSEPH

Order this book online at www.trafford.com
or email orders@trafford.com

Most Trafford titles are also available at major online book retailers.

Printed in the United States of America.

ISBN: 978-1-4269-9773-0 (sc)
ISBN: 978-1-4269-9774-7 (e)

Trafford rev. 11/18/2013

 www.trafford.com

North America & international
toll-free: 1 888 232 4444 (USA & Canada)
fax: 812 355 4082

PREFACE

BY

JAMES J. PILGRIM, DDS, FICD

As a member of St. Joseph's Episcopal Church, in Fayetteville, North Carolina, I have had the opportunity and pleasure of hearing many of Father Augustine Joseph's poems which he penned for special occasions such as Mother's Day and Black History Month. He has always delivered his poems in a balanced manner so that all listeners could appreciate the message he was trying to get across.

The readers of this book, will thoroughly enjoy the poems and his interpretation of many major events that we are facing today as well as several biblical stories. From the beginning the reader is introduced to the work of the poet in general. In the Book of Genesis, the readers will delve into the Story of Adam & Eve in the Garden of Eden. Father Joseph later deals with a wide cross section of poems including The Kingships of David and Solomon, in Solomon, Israel's Wisest King, as well as some New Testament stories.

Relative to contemporary times, Father Joseph deals with serious and significant issues of our times. Included among them are The Election of President Barack Obama, Obama, Yes We Can, Dr. Martin Luther King, Jr., and the Egyptian Revolution. Many of us will be able to relate for personal reasons to the poems. The Homeless, Gasoline Too High, The Networks and Stop the Bully, because unfortunately these are the issues we are faced with daily. For better or worse he has composed poetry that faces these growing realities of our times.

INTRODUCTION

I am a Priest who was trained at Codrington College, Barbados. There, I obtained the B.A. in Theology, and the Licentiate in Theology (L. Th). At the time, this was done in conjunction with the University of the West Indies. Since then, I have served in parishes in Trinidad and Tobago, Barbados, and in the United States. I am married to my dear wife, Barbara Walcott of Barbados, and we were blessed with four children, namely, Anthony, Ryan, Nicolas and Barbara-Anne.

First, I want to thank the members of the churches in which I served, including my present church, St. Joseph's Episcopal, Fayetteville, North Carolina. These members encouraged me to publish my sermons.

I told them that I would, but I never thought that a book of poems would be first.

I first started to write poems at about the age of seven, when I won a first prize at my elementary school, at St. David, Toco, Trinidad, W.I. And I continued writing from time to time. When I emigrated to the U.S. in 1987, my interest in the art continued. But it became more prominent, when I became the rector of St. Joseph's in 1991. Over the years, I have achieved many awards in poetry writing, including the Shakespearian Award in Hollywood, California in 2003. My first publication was a poem called: "Unwelcomed Invitation: Snow Storm 2000." My second publication was a poem entitled, "The Poet" which was put to music by a Country Singer, in Nashville, T.N. I opened the book with it, because it sums up the work of the poet.

The idea for the book came as a flash of inspiration one day while driving. "Why not write Bible stories in Poetry, and add some contemporary topics to it?" Hence the title of the book! It is my hope, that you, the reader, will read the Bible passages associated with the poems. This will add to your Bible reading and knowledge, as well as make you very conversant with the text.

Special thanks to Mrs. Karen Washington, Ms. Bernice Motley, Mrs. Jan Mumford, and Mrs. Lerlene Walcott, for helping with some of the typing. I really appreciate it. A special thanks also to my wife, Barbara, who was an inspiration to me in writing the book. This book should have a world-wide appeal, as there is something there for everyone. Similarly, Christians throughout the world, should find it helpful.

I hope you, the reader, would enjoy it, as much as I enjoyed writing it.

Augustine Joseph

THE POET

There is no subject out of reach
Of which the poet's words cannot speak
With roving eyes and pensive mind,
The poet plumbs deeply humankind.

No one's too poor to catch his gaze
No one's too rich to be amazed
Topics flow freely in his mind
In single verse or with a rhyme.

The poet can lift a weary soul,
There are so many in this world,
Provide the words, lighten their load,
Send them reflecting on life's road

Some write of religion and faith
That lifts men's souls to Heaven's gate
Some write of nature as divine,
Dumbfounded by its grand design

Great admiration for his work,
His words stand like a giant oak.
Poets do bring sunshine to our face
Without them, poorer is our race.
Augustine Joseph

THE BIBLE

(1) The Bible is a library and God's holy Book
It's too important for anyone to overlook
Its message is God's love and salvation
Reaching out to all cultures and every nation.

(2) The Gospels of Matthew, Mark, Luke, and John,
Tell how Jesus' ministry got off the ground.
He chose twelve disciples as fishers of men.
And he promised to be with them to the end.

(3) God's word is living and active, sharper than a sword.
It mentions in Hebrews, God's holy record.
Every word written there is inspired by God.
So that all will confess, Jesus Christ as Lord.

(4) It has Old Testament history, parables and more.
Its teachings inspire, all ages for sure.
The epistles and gospels convey the good news.
God's message to the world, was first sent to the Jews.

(5) God sent his Son Jesus Christ to save the lost,
He came, and died for us on the cross.
Anyone who accepts, Jesus' salvation,
Would experience in the end, his resurrection.

(6) The first book of Genesis tells how all things began
With the creative power of God's Almighty hand.
The last book of Revelation says it like a refrain
That Jesus, The Messiah, is coming again!

XXX

THE AMAZING CREATOR

GENESIS 1: 1-9

From the beginning God has always been there
Long before there were any birds in the air.
God is the only infinite Being
The only creator of all human beings.

At first God created the heavens and the earth.
It was empty and dark like a child blind at birth.
Nothing lived on the earth; there was no life on it.
Until God gave it life with His moving spirit.

God said, "Let there be light," and there was light,
Then everything glowed, luminously and bright.
He called the light Day; it was just like day light.
And the darkness he gave, no other name but Night.

God spoke again, and he made the open sky
With an amazing blue color, it stood very high.
God called the land to appear on the scene,
And not very long after, it would become very green.

God called the land 'Earth', and that was its name.
But the waters of the Sea were far from the same.
God looked at His work from the place where he stood,
And "Behold," he said, "It was very good."

God called the plants to appear out of the ground,
For before not a single plant was around.
Then the sun and the moon were ordered in the sky.
By the Creator, with whom no other being could vie.

THE FIFTH DAY OF CREATION

On the fifth day God spoke from on high,
"I want the seas filled with fish, and birds in the sky."
God created everything for our livelihood,
"And Behold!" he said, "It was very good."

Then all kinds of animals came, and inhabit the land,
From the smallest to the greatest, that are stronger than man.
All kinds of trees to make firewood
"And Behold" God said, "It was very good."

Then God said, "Now I am going to create human beings
To rule the earth and every creature that's seen
He will be superior, to all living things."
For the Lord has given to him, special blessings.

So God gathered together some dust of the ground,
And formed it into a man to be very strong,
God breathe the breath of life into him
And man became a human being, for daily uplifting.

ADAM & EVE

On the fifth day, God spoke again from on high.
"I want the sea filled, and many birds in the sky."
God created everything for our livelihood.
And, "behold", he said, "it was very good."

All kinds of animals inhabit the land.
From the smallest to the biggest, stronger than man.
With all kinds of trees to make firewood.
And, "behold," God said, "it was very good."

Then God said, "I am going to create human beings.
To rule over the earth, and every creature that's seen.
They will be superior to all other living things.
For I am giving to them a very special blessing."

So God gathered together, some dust from the ground.
And formed it into a man to be wise and strong.
So God breathed the breath of life into him.
And man became more than a living thing!

God saw that Adam, was in a lonely state,
So he thought of getting him a desired helpmate.
He put Adam to rest in a very deep sleep.
And took one of his ribs, for the woman to keep.

The rib, he put into the woman he made.
She was a partner to him and never a maid.
To the woman, he gave the name of Eve.
And with her, the man, Adam, was very pleased.

XXXX

PUT IN BUT DRIVEN OUT

ADAM, IN AND OUT OF THE GARDEN
GENESIS 2:8-24

The good Lord had created the very first man
And gave him the masculine name of Adam,
Soon after God planted a lovely garden
In a beautiful place, called the Garden of Eden.

The garden was huge with rich soil deposit,
As four big rivers did flow through it.
And beautiful foliage did grow all around,
Some serving as food to make Adam strong.

God put him in charge of the garden to care,
He must till it, and prune it, for his own welfare.
God had given to man such a picturesque place
It's one of those gifts one cannot replace.

On the fourth day God spoke from on high
"Let the sun, moon, and stars come into the sky."
And as the Lord said he wanted them there
Each one came out, and in the sky appear.

The moon and the stars were, to give light at night
And the sun with it's brilliance, to give daily light
What a beautiful world, and a bright neighborhood
"For Behold," the Lord said, "It was very good."

God laid down the rules for Adam to obey.
There were two trees to be aware of everyday.
The tree of life, emanated a spirit of good will
And the tree of knowledge to know good and evil.

God warned Adam, "Don't eat from the "knowledge" tree.
But Eve, by her action, did disagree!
She picked one of the fruits, and gave Adam piece to eat.
He tasted it and said it was very sweet.

From that moment they knew they were both naked.
They covered themselves, and with leaves they hid.
Then God came and called, "Adam, where are you?"
And Adam said, "We are naked, but we never knew."

God said, "Who told you, you were naked? That's really
The truth.
Did you disobey, and help yourself with a fruit?"
"The woman you gave me, picked it from the tree,
And told me to taste it, as an endorsee."

But God drove them out of the garden that day.
There was nothing worthwhile, they could really say.
God had warned them before, not to eat of the fruit
The only choice left, was to give them the boot!

XXXX

"CAIN & ABEL"

GENESIS 3: 23-4: 16

Cain and Abel were born to Adam and Eve
But Cain his jealousy couldn't quell or appease.
Cain was happy, producing the fruits of the land
While Abel preferred tending after the lamb.

Cain offered to God some of the fruits of the land.
But God didn't accept it; Cain didn't understand.
Abel offered his lamb as a people on the move,
And for this, the good Lord didn't disapprove.

Maybe, Israel as a people had to move on in haste,
And couldn't afford to settle down in any one place.
Abel's gift was acceptable to God at the time.
For farming would have put Israel deep in a bind.

But Cain became jealous over his brother Abel,
And Cain struck him down in the field where he fell.
God called and asked Cain for his only brother,
But Cain replied, that he wasn't his brother's keeper.

God said, "Abel's blood cried out to me, out of the ground.
In a painfully tragic and mournful sound."
God said, Cain must answer for his sin, clandestine,
And for the very first murder, a horrible crime.

"NOAH BUILDS AN ARK"

GENESIS 6:1-7:5

God looked at the world and was very displeased.
The people were wicked and caused him to grieve.
God was very sorry with the state of the world
And planned to destroy the human race as a whole.

But there was one righteous man, who was living God's way.
And he and his family didn't have to pay.
God directed Noah to build an Ark.
For all life will drown when the heavy rains start.

The Ark was the size of a three storey building.
Big enough, with the capacity for safely floating.
Noah must put a pair of each animal safely inside.
For the Ark would survive every rising tide.

Noah was to store enough food up for everybody.
In case of any unforeseen eventuality.
And after all the animals have been placed inside before,
He and his family must then lock the door.

In seven days God will pour down heavy rain on the earth.
Not one thing will live that ever gave birth.
It would rain forty days and forty nights.
Before the skies appear once more sunny and bright.

"NOAH"

GENESIS 7: 6-8:19

Noah was 600 years old when the rain clouds did burst.
He was locked in the Ark but expected the worst.
The rain poured on the earth as never before.
The waters rose up outside, very close to the door.

It rained forty long days and forty nights.
And afterwards outside became sunny and bright.
God let out a dove to see what it would meet.
It came back later, with an olive leaf in its beak.

So Noah knew that the earth was drying out very fast.
He was happy that the rain had stopped at last.
God told Noah to bring everyone out of the Ark.
They could go and play safely some where in the park.

"RAINBOW PROMISE"

Genesis 8:20-9:17

The flood was over; everything was still,
Noah saw the bodies of the massive kill.
Not one life survived, except those in the Ark,
And now they were running around in the park.

Noah built an Altar and thanked God almighty,
For saving his life and his family.
God made a big promise after the flood came,
Not to destroy all life by flooding again.

The four seasons will come and the four seasons will go.
Every year that passes it will be so.
God said to Noah, "Take charge of the earth."
And treat it like one to whom he has given birth.

And like the bright star that traveled with the magi.
Behold a beautiful rainbow appeared in the sky
It was a sign to remind God, what he said of the rain;
"I would not destroy the earth by a flood again."

"GOD APPEARS TO ABRAHAM"

GENESIS 12: 1-13: 18

Once there was an ancient city by the name of Ur.
And God needed a man with whom to concur.
A man named Abraham, accustomed to his own pace.
God called him and said to him, "you must leave this place."

He must go to a land that God will show to him.
And Abraham was puzzled over such a thing.
God promised to bless him, and make his family great,
Though of humble beginnings and of low estate.

Abraham left with his family to an unknown land.
Setting out to a place he didn't understand.
But he had trust in God and decided to go.
"If God said it is so, then it will be so."

They crossed over rivers and hills to Canaan.
He was doing all this at the Lord's command
They camped at a big oak tree at Morch.
From there he listened to what the Lord had to say.

God spoke to him as a trusted friend,
"I will give this land to all your children."
Abraham built an altar and worshiped the Lord.
The one great Almighty, Omnipotent God.

GOD'S PROMISE TO ABRAHAM

GENESIS 15: 1-18

God came to Abraham again one night,
But the light that night was not very
Bright
"Don't be afraid Abraham," God said to
Him.
I have come here to tell you a wonderful
Thing!"

"I will protect you, and give you a
Great reward."
Abraham couldn't believe it, he was
So greatly awed.
"I am old," Abraham said "with no
Children of mine."
But God told him don't worry it will work
Out fine.

God took him outside to look up at the stars.
They were numerous and twinkling, smaller
Than Mars.
"Your children will be like the stars
Of heaven.
Canaan will be theirs, it's what I
Have given."

Abraham believed the Lord God, and
Did not doubt.
For God had the power to work all things
Out!
God described Abraham, as a man of faith.
It did not matter to him, how long he had
To wait.

XXXX

SARAH LAUGHS AT GOD

It was incredibly hot by the oaks of
Mamre.
And Abraham was sitting in the shade
That day.
Looking up, he saw God, and two angels
Nearby.
Although he was troubled, he didn't question
Why?

The party of three, all looked just like
Men.
So Abraham thought of entertaining them.
Abraham was going inside to prepare them
Some lunch.
To get them something on which they could
Munch.

"Where is your wife?" God asked Abraham.
"She is inside from the heat, it could kill
Any man!"
"I brought you some good news, it is
Now about noon.
Your dear wife, Sarah, will have a baby
Boy soon."

Sarah heard what was said, and began to
Laugh.
Which prompted the Lord to make a remark,
"Why did she laugh?" God asked Abraham.
"She is far too old," I don't see how she can!"

God said that nothing is impossible with Him
And both of them will witness this very thing.
"Tell Sarah she must not be a non-believer.
She will soon have a baby boy to Look after.

XXXX

SODOM ON FIRE

GENESIS 19: 1-24

While God spoke with Abraham, angels left Mamre.
They had other duties to carry out that day.
Lot sat outside next to Sodom's gate.
He was told, soon the city would disintegrate.

Sodom had become a wicked and sinful city.
And was sinking everyday in depravity.
The only remedy, and godly solution,
Was Sodom's total destruction and annihilation.

The angels told Lot, to leave straight-away and go.
He hesitated for a while, but he couldn't, say no.
Then the angels grabbed him firmly by the hand.
And told him to follow, it's the Lord's command.

They rushed him, his wife, and two daughters out!
"Run for your lives, please don't hold back or doubt.
What ever you do, just follow my track,
But please, I urge you, you must never look back!"

Sin is hateful to God, who we must not provoke.
Fire rained down on Sodom, with a choking smoke.
When we are obedient to God, he will surely exalt.
Lot's wife disobeyed, and became a pillar of salt.

XXXX

A FATAL MISTAKE

GENESIS 19

For both Sodom and Gomorrah, God's judgment had come
Those who heard the warning must pack up and run.
Yet Lot and his family still resided there.
But God sent his angel to help them and take care.

The angel told Lot he must leave right away,
Not the next day, or next week, but that very day,
Lot, however, hesitated and lingered till dawn,
But to wait any longer, he would regret he was born.

The angel grabbed them, including his two daughters all.
Time was running out, before the cities would fall
As they ran, falling sulpher began to unpack,
And the angel gave warning, no one should look back.

It was a hellish inferno, and no one there survived.
The smell and the smoke confirmed everyone died.
But Lot's wife couldn't resist to look back at the sight.
It was something so frightful, she looked back while in flight.

But what an awful mistake, she in an instant did make!
By disobeying, she had sealed her own fate.
She chose to look back; it was all her own fault.
And was turned instantly into a pillar of salt.

HE WAS TRICKED

GENESIS CHAPTER 39

A captive of Israelite's traders of the world
Joseph was taken to Egypt, where he was sold.
A man named Potiphar, high in the King's ranks,
Gave Joseph a position, for which he gave thanks.

He was still an attractive and very young man,
And Potiphar's wife tried to woo his hand.
She tried over and over, and wouldn't give up,
Although many times, Joseph told her to stop.

She tried to trick Joseph, and grabbed at his shirt,
But being young and agile, he was quick and alert.
He escaped by loosing his shirt in her grab,
Upset by his action, she was angry and mad.

She complained, Joseph was a man out of control,
"His actions," she said, "Was outrageously bold."
Potiphar, was furious, and and for good reason,
And had innocent Joseph, thrown into prison.

It is true the same things still happen today
Some would plan to ensnare you in any way.
It is best to do always, what is good and right.
And God will help you as you walk in the light.

XXXX

JOSEPH, THE DREAMER

GENESIS CHAPTER 40-41

Joseph became the chief servant to the Egyptian King,
Who had his wine stewart and chief baker worrying,
The King put them in prison, to await their fate,
Both were fearful of the King's execution date.

One night both men had a very strange dream
Each one was eager to know what his dream might mean.
The wine steward dreamt of squeezing grape juice from the tree,
And he wanted to know what the meaning might be.

Josephy told him that the King would reinstate him,
The good news, no doubt caused him to dance and sing.
Then the chief baker told Joseph about his dream
And couldn't wait to find out what his dream might mean.

He said, "I was carrying baskets of pastries for the King,
But birds came and ate them and left nothing for him."
Joseph told him that the meaning pointed to the dead,
"For in three days the King will sever his head."

The wine steward was happy he got back his job,
But the bad news for the chief baker, caused his heart to throb.
Disturbed over what Joseph, the dreamer had said,
As predicted, in three days, the King severed his head.

The King learned of Joseph's dream-solving skills,
For none of his wise men had the gift or the will.
The King wanted an answer to a puzzling dream,
He was fortunate to have Joseph, right there on the scene.

"I was standing," the King said, "by the River Nile.
When seven fat cows emerged in a short while,
Seven thin cows, in like fashion, also appeared,
Then I witnessed something gruesome, and very weird."

"The thin cows overpowered, and ate up the fat ones,
And never stopped eating until their meal was done.
He dreamt also of seven fully grown ripe ears of corn
Were devoured by other corn that was meager and drawn."

"Tell me Joseph," he said, "what's the interpretation here!
I can't solve it, for it is out of my sphere."
"God is sending a message to you," Joseph said.
There will be seven years of plenty and seven years with no bread."

Joseph told him, "put someone capable in charge
And the country's economy would once more recharge.
Everything from the smallest, will depend on him,
Do it, and you'll survive the far—reaching famine."

MOSES AND THE EXODUS

EXODUS CHAPTERS 2 TO 20

(1) Baby Moses, was born at a perilous time,
Baby boys were killed, and it wasn't a crime.
The midwives were ordered to take a baby boy's life
"Just withhold the oxygen; no need for a knife"

(2) Moses at his birth, was a handsome boy,
His mother understood not, those who planned to destroy.
She hid him at home, for three months for sure,
But after that time, it wasn't safe anymore.

(3) So she wove a strong basket, and put him it,
And took it down to the Nile, to safely deposit;
Then she hid the basket among the tall bulrushes,
Her handsome baby, to be known as Moses;

(4) Pharaoh's daughter, went down to the river to bathe,
"I hear a child crying! Someone get me an aid!"
She took the child safely, up to Pharaoh's palace,
There couldn't be a better location, for a hiding place.

(5) Moses, grew up, and went to the land of Midian;
And became a good shepherd and a responsible man;
But while he was grazing his flock on the range,
He saw a bush burning; it was very strange.

(6) The bush kept buring, but he couldn't explain,
So he turned to look at it again and again,
As he sought to find meaning form the rare attraction,
God called him, and he knew it was a revelation.

(7) The Lord called out to Moses, his voice very strong,
"Don't come any closer, you're on holy ground!
I am the God of Abraham, Isaac, and Jacob,
I need you to carry out a masterful job!"

(8) "I hear the cries of my people down in Egypt.
I need you to go down, and bring an end to it!
They're suffering at the hands of the heartless Pharaoh,
You must tell him, I say, 'let all my people go."

(9) "But he doesn't know me!" Moses expressed his doubt;
"And I'm sure he is going to drive me out!"
God said, "Tell him that I AM, THAT AM, have sent you,"
He is a hard-hearted man, let's see what he'll do."

(10) "And when he asks for your name, what then must I say?
Otherwise, he will certainly chase me away!"
God said, "Tell him, 'I AM, THAT I AM' have sent you.
But don't be alarmed, you don't know what he'll do."

(11) Then Moses, and Aaron, went before the king,
And told him that God said, "Put an end to this thing."
Pharaoh said, "Who is he? I would like to know,
But I'll never agree to let these people go!"

(12) God sent gnats, flies, and hail over Egypt's land,
But Pharaoh wouldn't agree to the Lord's command,
It took ten sets of plagues, before Pharaoh came to know,
That God wasn't joking, when He said, "Let them go."

(13) Finally, Moses told his people, 'Get a lamb, a year old,
Each family must kill it, and do exactly as told."
They must sprinkle the blood, on the doorframes of each house,
And a destroying angel will leave them out.

(14) "But the Egyptians will suffer a terrible blow.
For the angel will kill the first born as they go;"
Then Egyptians beg the Hebrews to hurry up and leave,
Their anguish was intense, they started to grieve.

(15) Then Moses and his people, left Egypt and depart,
At first, they did nothing, before they were told to start.
But when Pharaoh realized it wasn't a dream but a fact,
He sent his chariots and horsemen, to bring them back.

(16) The Egyptians left racing; and were hot on their heel.
As though the feet of the horses, were protected with steel,
But the Israelites, were hemmed in, totally by the Red Sea,
And that threatened their escape and liberty!

(17) But Moses stretched his hand out, in the presence of all,
And the waters divided; on each side like a wall,
Then the dry land appeared; and the people crossed over,
It all seemed to be part of the great Passover.

(18) The Egyptians try to follow, but they went into shock,
As the returning waters became Egypt's stumbling-block
And all the Egyptians were drowned in the marvelous Red Sea;
Moses knew it was God, who gave the victory.

(19) They roamed in the wilderness for a long forty years,
And their stubborn life-style brought Moses next to tears.
The hungry people complained that it didn't worth it,
For though things were bad, they had food in Egypt!

(20) But in the evening, God provided quails for them to eat,
They covered the camp all around their feet.
And in the morning, they had something else that was God-given,
The Lord provided manna for them from heaven.

(21) When the people reached the Desert of Mount Sinai,
There was thunder and lightning, and some questioned why?
Then Moses, led them from the camp to meet with God,
God had something to say, as their Creator and Lord.

(22) From the top of Mount Sinai, he called Moses alone up,
And God gave Ten Commandments, they all must adopt.
They tell us how to serve God and relate with Him,
And how to treat our neighbor, a fellow pilgrim!

(23) Moses was Israel's liberator and law-giver,
Inspiring his people to follow their Creator;
From a wayward brood, living a life of reproach,
He transformed from rabble-rousers into a church.

Xxxxxxxxxxxxxxxx

THE ABC'S OF MOTHERS

AUGUSTINE JOSEPH

A—Mothers are like angels: they're always watching over you.

B—Mothers are like Bibles: they impart godly wisdom each day.

C—Mothers are like cookbooks: they give instructional recipes for life.

D—Mothers are like doctors: they'll work on your heart if they have to.

E—Mothers are like engineers: they'll make a way to your goals in life.

F—Mothers are like feet: they'll show you the different walks of life.

G—Mothers are like generals: they'll go to war to protect you.

H—Mothers are like hospitals: no wonder you call them Doctor Mom.

I—Mothers are like injections: sometimes the hurt is for your good.

J—Mothers are like Jesus: salvation is their main concern.

K—Mothers are like knowledge: they hold the key to your future.

L—Mothers are like lighthouses: they'll warn you of the pitfalls of life.

M—Mothers are like Mary: they ponder over the meaning of their kids.

N—Mothers are like newspapers: they always have news for you.

O—Mothers are like an orchestra: they'll help you attain a standing ovation.

P—Mothers are like prayers: they talk to God on your behalf.

Q—Mothers are like questions: they'll help you find an answer even if you think you already have one.

R—Mothers are like radios: they want to know whom you're listening to.

S—Mothers are like statesmen: they rock the cradle and stabilize the world.

T—Mothers are like telephones: they're always available to talk.

U—Mothers are like universities: they'll go to any degree for your success.

V—Mothers are like vice-presidents: they're very important people.

W—Mothers are like writers: they can produce volumes on your life story.

X—Mothers are like Xerox: there is much you can copy from them.

Y—Mothers are like yearbooks: they always have memories of you.

Z—Mothers are like zeros: they're indispensable to your life, as Y2K is to the new millennium.

"WE WANT A KING"

1 SAMUEL 8; 1-22

Their enemies, the Philistines gave Israel a blow
Stealing the Ark of the Covenant, Israel cried "NO!"
But seven months later, they returned the Ark.
An event that left Israel an occasion to mark

Samuel judged Israel in a time of peace.
The Lord caused all disputes and war to cease.
Most of the people decided to serve the Lord.
But others had influences from abroad.

"You're growing very old and your sons can't rule well.
Look at what they have done! Everyone can tell.
We all want a king, like the other nations."
They shouted out to Samuel, in affirmation.

But Samuel felt they wanted, to desert the Lord.
Something he felt passionately, he couldn't afford.
But the Lord said to Samuel, "Give them what they wish.
It would turn out to be an unpleasant dish."

"So don't you worry Samuel, on the contrary.
It's no rejection of you, but rejection of me."
Samuel listed the negatives, the monarchy will bring.
But the people still shouted: "We want our own king."

So the Lord told Samuel, "Give them what they asked.
They would soon want to return to the days of the past.
So give them a king and send them away.
It wouldn't be long before they all start to pay."

"GOD CHOOSES A KING

1 SAMUEL 9 : 1-25

Saul, a very handsome man was on his father's errand.
His father's donkeys, had escaped from his hand
So Saul and his servants went in search after them.
He wondered if they had fallen into the enemies hand

After searching the landscape from place to place.
Saul decided to turn back and returned to base.
But his servants said to him, while they were still in Zuph.
"We have searched all over and have had enough."

"There is a man of God here, we should see him first."
This would be for the better, and not for the worst"
Meanwhile, the Lord had told Samuel that Saul was coming.
And Saul and his servants went looking for him.

Some girls had the knowledge, where the seer could be found.
"Just ask as you go, he's very near around."
Saul unknowingly met Samuel and ask eagerly,
Where Samuel could be found in the vicinity.

"I am Samuel, the man you're looking for.
Your search is now over, so look no more.
Israel is looking to you as their very first King.
Even though you are a man hailed from Benjamin."

But Saul replied to Samuel discouragingly.
"I'm from a small tribe and small family."
But Samuel won't accept "no" for an answer.
For Saul would be crowned king, sooner, than later.

"SAUL IS ANOINTED"

1 SAMUEL 9: 26-10:27

Early the next morning, they were on their feet.
Both Samuel and Saul walked into the street.
Samuel sent on Saul's servant ahead of them.
He didn't want him to see what would follow then.

Samuel poured a small flask of oil over Saul's head.
"God told me to anoint you as King of Israel.
Some people and events you'll meet on the way.
These are clear signs that God has chosen you today."

"As you travel you'll first come to Rachel's tomb.
There good news awaits you, it couldn't come too soon.
Two men have the news, that the donkeys are safe.
And your father is now looking for you in their place."

"As you go you'll meet three men on the way.
They'll greet you, and offer you loaves without pay.
Accept them and proceed without any delay.
You'll meet musical prophets, spirit-filled as they play."

"You too would be rapt like a prophet of God.
Do not worry because it is the work of the Lord."
So as Saul was leaving and about to depart.
God gave him a new and inspired heart.

Then some others burst out in prophetic singing.
For the spirit of God took possession of him.
This wasn't his style, and he would first admit it.
And some asked: "Is Saul also among the prophets?"

After 300 years under the judges leadership.
Israel for the first time had its own kingship.
It was a new institution, never tried before.
They had to adjust to the administration of law.

SAUL BECOMES KING

SAUL: THE FIRST KING

Samuel became judge of all Israel.
His service had wonderful stories to tell.
He proclaimed the Lord's message, that was tried and true.
And told the people that they had to do.

With the passage of time, Samuel grew very old
He couldn't as before, do a hundred fold.
He put his two sons, to be judge in his place.
With corruption they turned out to be a disgrace.

The people wanted Israel to be ruled by a King,
Samuel told them it would be a lamentable thing.
But they wanted a King like the other nations.
It would bring an end, to Samuel's sons corruption.

God told Samuel, to warn them of the demands of a king.
He would cause the people undue suffering.
But the people were unwavering in having their way.
God said, "Let them have it, they'd remember this day."

So Saul was chosen to be Israel's first King.
Oil was poured on his head for the great anointing.
Samuel told the people that God had chosen him.
And the people all shouted, "God save the King!"

THE AMMONITES ATTACK

1 Samuel 11: 1-12, 25

It was a month, since Saul was anointed King.
And something occurred that offended him.
The Ammonites attacked Israel, at Jabesh.
And the people of Israel were shell-shocked by this.

Wailing and crying were heard everywhere.
The lament of the nation was too much to bear.
When news of the attack reached the ears of young Saul
He was aroused with anger and couldn't rest at all.

The spirit of God suddenly came upon him
And felt a consuming fire from within.
He killed and dissected Oxen in many pieces.
And sent them around Israel to invoke responses.

Saul's message was clear, you must come out and fight.
The nation must mobilize and show its real might.
"Join me now, and let's fight off the invading Ammonites
Or both you and your Oxen will be like this gruesome sight."

Over 300,000 (three hundred thousand) soldiers joined Saul on that
day.
And despoil the Ammonites in total disarray.
Samuel called all the people to assemble at Gilgal.
And he gave Saul the kingdom and bid them farewell.

He told them he would always pray on their behalf.
The must serve the Lord totally and not in part.
"If you serve him faithfully, all will be well, I say,
Or else you and your king will be all swept away."

SAUL FELL FROM FAVOR

1 Samuel 13: 1-14

They hoped Saul was their answer to the Philistines threat
But after two years the people started to fret,
Saul's army overran the Philistines at Geba
But that wasn't enough to repel them forever.

They re-grouped and became even stronger than before,
And Israel had an enemy right at their door.
Thus the Philistines became Israel's formidable foe;
But how to defeat them, Saul really didn't know.

Saul blasting his trumpet, called his men out to war
But many were afraid and didn't fight as before!
They came, but came with intimidation and fear.
The recipe for disaster was in the air.

Samuel was delayed for a sacrifice prior to the war.
And Saul's men were impatiently going through the door.
After seven days, Saul decided to substitute for him.
Samuel called it a blunder; an objectionable thing.

"My men were leaving." Saul to Samuel said.
So I offered the sacrifice after waiting instead.
I was afraid that the Philistines would come and attack.
And hurt us to the point where we couldn't fight back."

Samuel insisted that Saul had done something very wrong.
"Not easily corrected for what you're done.
So God will find another to fill in your place,
Because now you have fallen into disgrace."

GOD RIPS AWAY THE KINGDOM

1 SAMUEL 15: 1-35

Despite the many troubles that the young King Saul had.
He defeated Israel's enemies even though a young lad.
But there was one more opponent, strong like the Hittities
And that was the dreaded Amalekites.

God wanted him to defeat them once and for all.
The Amalekites army must completely fall.
So Saul defeated and conquered their cherished places,
But foolishly saved animals for sacrifices.

When Samuel heard of it, he was very upset.
And over Saul's kingship, he had serious regret.
What god needed from Saul, was complete obedience.
And anything less was a great offence.

Samuel told Saul that God had rejected him.
And he would find someone else to replace him as King.
As Samuel turned to depart, Saul grabbed on to his robe.
And it ripped from the shoulders as Samuel was in strode.

Samuel saw it as symbolic of God's command.
That he had ripped the kingdom out of his hand.
"From now on, you Saul must fully understand.
God is giving your kingship to a better man."

THE SHEPHERD BOY ANOINTED

1 SAMUEL 16:1-12

The word of the Lord came to Samuel
Again:
"I want one of Jesse's sons as king to reign.
So bring some oil to Bethlehem.
For the kingship is going to one of them."
When he arrived he made a sacrifice to
God.
To keep him focused on the work of the Lord.
Meanwhile, Jesse and his seven sons were
All there.
And the Lord told Samuel to have a listening
Ear.
"None of the seven will be appointed Saul's
Heir:
So don't be too quick to anoint any of them
There."
They were handsome and attractive,
And seemed very smart
But the Lord said to Samuel, "first look
At the heart!"
"Are these all of your sons?" Samuel said to Jesse.
"There is one with the sheep but he is not
Yet ready."
"The one in the field is too young for
A King.
So we need not all, should consider him."
"Send for him!" Samuel said," and bring
Him to me.

For this young shepherd boy, I must certainly
See."
He too was handsome with bright and clear eyes;
Not knowing Israel's kingship he was
Surely to rise.
When David arrived, God said, "This is
The one!"
Samuel's search for a king was over and
Done.
Samuel reached for the oil, and poured
It on him,
And the people once more had another king.

XXXX

MUSIC & THE MONARCHY

1 Samuel 16: 13-23

David was only a teenager at that very time.
He had rosy cheeks and was looking fine;
He was anointed in the presence of his others
Brothers.
As well as in the company of a few
Others.
Then the spirit of the Lord came mightily
Upon him.
A gift that he needed especially being king
The spirit was with him from that very
Hour;
And Samuel returned to his place at Ramah.
Meanwhile, Saul was tormented with an evil
Spirit;
But he did not have the answer to get rid
Of it.
But one of Saul's servants had a unique
Solution,
For Saul's violent mood swings and
Tormentation.
He suggested that David play sweetly on the harp
Strings.
He should be invited to come play for him.
The soothing music would surely compose his heart
And the wicked spirit will take leave and
Depart.
The suggestion pleased Saul and he sent for David
But unaware that his successor was right before him;
And David, not long thereafter, would ascend to the
Throne.
And Israel would be blessed with a good king of their own.

THE ANOINTED WARRIOR

1 Samuel 17: 1-45

In Saul's reign, the Philistines were a
Thorn in the flesh.
An now David must face them the
First time afresh.
Especially Goliath, who was nine
Feet tall.
He was a fearful and intimidating figure
To all.
He challenged all Israel to come and
Fight with him.
He told them, they had no one to come into the
'ring'.
Meanwhile Saul and his men had
To listen to him.
As he beat on his chest with arrogant
Boasting!
Saul and his army were somewhat
Afraid.
And hoped that the Lord God would come
To their aid.
The Philistines continued to poke fun at
Them.
Yet Israel saw victory but couldn't say
When.
When David heard that Goliath was sending
Out his challenge.
He was angry and fearless without a cringe
In defense of his kingdom he couldn't

Remiss.
And on hearing Goliath, he asked: "Who is this?"
David was ready to fight at God's
Faithful command.
With only a sling shot in his little
Hand.
He said to Goliath "You come
With your sword."
"But I will defeat you in the name
Of the Lord."

XXXX

DAVID RAN FOR THE CAVES

1 Samuel 17: 57-22:5

David came with Goliath's head in his hand,
The biggest war trophy achieved in the land.
Saul wouldn't allow David to return to his house,
Thank God, he did not yet have a spouse!

Saul's son and David became bosom friends.
They made a compact, but no signing with pens.
Jonathan's love for David was of a high degree
They'll protect each other in adversity.

Meanwhile, Saul and David couldn't get along,
Especially, when some women sang their victory song,
On David's victorious return over the Philistines,
The women came singing with tambourines and rhymes.

"Saul was able to make havoc of thousands;" they sang,
But David achieved more with a bigger bang!"
This tribute to David infuriated Saul,
It was bitter to him, more than the taste of gall.

Saul's hatred increased at a rapid pace,
David had to make sure of a hiding place
He soon afterwards, had to be on the run,
His men were hungry, and that was no fun!

They finally sought refuge in Adullam's caves
Where the poor and the troubled mixed with the brave.
They offered their services to fight with David.
But on hearing of Saul's death, he no longer hid.

DAVID SPARES SAUL

1 SAMUEL 24: 1-22

Among the rocks of the wild goats, David went into hide.
In one of the caves he went deep down inside.
But surprisingly, Saul came and fell asleep there,
And was at the mercy of David, he hadn't a prayer.

"He is a dead duck," David men said to him.
But David refused to hurt the Lord's anointed.
"Don't spare his life!" David's men won't give in.
But David still refused to hurt Israel's King.

David crept up and cut off piece of his coat,
And watched from a distance when Saul awoke.
David called out, and waved the piece in the air,
And said, "I didn't hurt you Saul because I care."

Saul was moved, by David's act of love.
And wished him well from the Lord above.
He was impressed and predicted what God did foretell,
That David would be King over Israel.

SAUL INVOKES SAMUEL

1 Samuel 28: 3-19; 2 Samuel 1-27
1 Samuel 31: 1-12

In the passage of time, Samuel died and went home.
And Saul was now old, and could no longer roam.
He wished that he had Samuel as a mentor
Because trouble was brewing very close to his door.

The Philistines were equipped to war against Israel.
And Saul was afraid and had no one to tell.
He learned of a psychic who spoke to the dead
He did ask the Lord, but got silence instead.

But Saul needed a quick answer with a plan to apply.
He couldn't understand why the Lord didn't reply.
He wanted the psychic to consult with Samuel.
So he traveled to Endor in disguised apparel.

He told her he needed help since he was down.
She said, she saw an old man coming up from the ground.
Samuel quarreled with Saul for disturbing his rest.
"And it was far too late now, to redirect the process."

"With the Philistines' threat tell me what must I do?"
Samuel told him: "God had rejected you!"
"Tomorrow you and your sons will be here with me.
It's only a matter of hours before this tragedy comes through."

The next day was a great battle on Mount Gilboa.
David learned of the news of the massive slaughter.
And Saul and his sons had perished in the fight.
The prediction of Samuel was exactly right.

David and his men wept over the loss.
It was too much to bear such a heavy cost.
Saul had been king just about 15 years.
And it came to an end with blood, sweat and tears.

THE VICTORIOUS KING

2 Samuel 5: 1-25

Long after Saul had died, David still wasn't King
Seven years had passed and no enthrone-ment of him
Whatever the reason, we are not clearly told.
But he wasn't made King till he was thirty years old.

Again the Philistines attacked the people of Israel.
And David prayed to the Lord, before launching ahead.
"Go around behind them," was God's advice to the King.
This took place near the valley of Rephaim.

"You'll hear a marching sound about in the treetops.
"This means I'll defeat them there on the spot."
And the Philistines armies were crushed on that day
One hundred years of war, came to an end that way.

A HAPPY DANCER

2 SAMUEL 6: 1-23

During Saul's reign, it was a different day.
The Ark of the Covenant was hidden away.
David planned to take it to Jerusalem,
There couldn't be a better site than on Mt. Zion.

An Ox-cart was built solely to carry the Ark.
A procession followed closely from the very start.
They made music and danced to their hearts content.
To the time when the priests took it into the tent.

Offerings were burned and offered to the Lord.
And the people were joyful and in one accord.
David was happily dancing before the Lord.
There was music and harmony without a discord.

DAVID'S HEART DEVOTED TO GOD

2 SAMUEL 7: 1-29

Jerusalem became known as the City of David.
It earned its name because of what David did.
Daily sacrifices were offered at the tabernacle.
So that Israel would be peaceful, strong and stable.

God's worship in the past left much to be desired.
And David wanted God's house to be one to be admired.
He remarked that he lived in a house of cedar.
And God's house, in a tent, deserved something better.

That night, God spoke to Nathan about the building plan.
But only David has the heart to build, and he can.
He sent word to tell David, that he gave him great power.
But his son will build him a house forever

URIAH'S DEATH

2 SAMUEL 11: 1-27

When David first became King he fought the enemy.
He remained in the palace, but knew the strategy.
One day while he stroll on the palace roof.
He saw someone that required a second look.

An attractive woman was taking a walk,
And David was amazed at what his eyes caught.
"Who is this woman?" He asked enquiringly
"She is not available! She belongs to somebody."

This is what David's servant had said to him.
But he felt otherwise being leader and king.
He was told that her name was lovely Bathsheba.
The wife of a soldier and Officer, Uriah.

David devised a wicked and sinister plan
Because he wanted to have Bathsheba's hand
Uriah was engaged in a war at the time
And David put him to fight in the firing line.

He wrote a letter to Joab, the general of the war,
Telling him to re-arrange the battle floor,
It was obvious David wanted Uriah's life,
So that he would be free, to have Bathsheba as his wife.

Joab followed David's orders and Uriah was grilled;
And soon there after, the soldier was killed.
Bathsheba mourned for her husband her dear valentine,
And David sent for her saying, "Bathsheba, now you're mine."

David and Bathsheba became husband and wife.
But God held it against David for Uriah's life.
God sent his prophet Nathan to confront the King.
For planning and committing such a terrible sin.

David was sorry and repented for what he had done.
We believe he was the writer of Psalm 51
God's way he would follow and henceforth impart.
To be described sometime later, "A man after God's own heart."

"YOU ARE THE MAN"

2 SAMUEL 12: 1-14

God sent his prophet, Nathan on an urgent mission.
He must confront David for what he had done.
God is no respecter of persons, whether peasant or King.
We must all give an account, surely, one day to Him.

So Nathan went to David about his infraction.
Nathan caused him to listen with wrapped attention.
He told him a story; he sat up in his chair.
And David concluded, the rich man was unfair.

Nathan told him of two men, one rich and one poor.
The poor man had one lamb: the rich man had more.
The poor man's one lamb grew with him like a kid.
For anyone to take it, David said, "God forbid!"

But one day the rich man had a special dinner.
He was host to a very special visitor.
But the lamb that he killed was not one of his own.
It was the one dear lamb taken from the poor man's home!

David was so angry, he couldn't contain himself.
He could have killed the rich man with bare hands himself.
"That man must die!" David said with command
And Nathan pointed to David and said, "You are the man!"

A LIFE GOES, A LIFE COMES

A Death & A Life
2 Samuel 12: 13-24

Nathan's rebuke, shocked and saddened David.
"I've sinned against the Lord, by what I did."
"God has forgiven you, I believe," Nathan said.
"But your child with Bathsheba would soon be dead."

The baby was ill one day less a week,
And David was restless, he couldn't eat or sleep.
He paced up and down praying for the child.
But on the seventh day his, and Bathsheba's baby died.

Hearing of the death, David got washed and dressed.
"I can't bring back my child," an obvious truth he confessed.
"I will certainly go to meet him, some day I'm sure.
But he'll never come back to me any more."

David and Bathsheba had another child.
He would impact Israel's history for a very long while.
Nathan, the prophet, named him Jedidiah.
But he was known by the name by his father.

David preferred to name his son, Solomon
We will learn of his great wisdom before long.
He was one of the wisest Kings of Israel.
The records are there, anyone can tell.

Nathan predicted that David's household would suffer.
For the murder of officer Uriah.
And Nathan's prediction began to materialize.
For many of his sons led unruly lives.

David's son Absalom had long, beautiful hair,
But who really knows what lies in the air?
One day Absalom rode swiftly in the breeze.
And his hair got entangled high up in the trees.

He was left swinging there helplessly in the oak,
And Joah was serious; It was no time for a joke.
Absalom could do nothing, hanging up in the air.
He was killed by Joab, an archer; with a spear.

DAVID'S SINFUL DEED

2 Samuel 24 1-25
1 Chronicle 21: 1-27

David ordered Joab to count the people.
But God viewed David's actions as objectionable.
Joab knew it was wrong but did it anyway,
For the King overruled him, he had no lee way.

The Lord disliked intensely, what David had done,
But the act was completed, it couldn't be undone.
God sent a disease, seventy thousand of them died,
And those who survived it lamented and cried.

A destroying angel targeted Jerusalem,
As for the people it seemed nothing could save them.
But God said to the angel, "Enough, do no more!"
As the angel was close to the trashing floor.

David obediently offered a sacrifice there.
And the site was ear-marked for the house of prayer.
Araunah offered to David, the land free and clear,
But the King didn't accept it and paid what was fair.

DAVID RUNS AND HIDES AGAIN

2 SAMUEL 13: 1-15

He was bitterly angry with his half
Brother Ammon.
For the violence of Tamar which he had
Done.
Absalom concealed his anger till an
Appropriate time.
He was planning revenge for an act out
Of line.
Absalom gave a feast; David's sons were
There.
Ammon was most present, he couldn't miss
The affair.
But while they were feasting, Absalom
Gave the sign
For his men to attack Ammon, for his sister's
Crime.
Meanwhile, the others started to run for
Their lives.
Things happened so quicly, it took them by
Surprise.
When the news got to David, he tore his
Clothes and mourn
Over Ammon's death, he was distressed
And thorn.
But David loved Absalom the most of all
Three years later his sons, came back to call.
Absalom was ambitious like Saladin,
He assembled a group and declared himself

King.
His outrage left David alarmed and amazed.
That his son would do anything for the power he
Craved.
So David and his household went
Into hiding.
For Absalom would have killed him, just to be king.
But Joab and his men had to protect
The King,
Even though it meant for David, intense
Suffering.
It was moaning and groaning on David's
Part.
As his son Absalom received three spears
To the heart.

XXXX

ABSALOM'S DEATH

2 Samuel 17:24-18:33

David found a safe place in the hills of Gilead.
With a very small army that he himself led.
Though small, his militia was daringly brave.
David and his household they were out to save.

As they marched out to fight in those days without gun.
David pleaded, "Be gentle with my son Absalom."
The battle was gruesome and bloody that day.
About 20,000 fell or perished in the fray.

When Absalom realized that his defeat was near,
He rode away quickly, for he hadn't a prayer.
But his hair got entangled in a branch of the trees.
He was left hanging helplessly in the breeze.

Joab had three spears, when he found Absalom.
Swinging above his head in isolation.
We don't know what he said to Joab on his part.
But Joab released the three spears straight to his heart.

He was cut down from the oak and thrown into a pit.
A huge heap of stones were placed over it.
David saw a runner in haste from the city gates.
"He's coming I'm sure, with the battle up-dates."

"Is Absalom safe?" David haltingly said,
But the runner replied: "Everyone was dead."
And David's lament was heart felt to the core;
He couldn't bear the anguish and grief anymore.

His words are here quoted without paraphrase.
So that you feel what he felt in those horrible days.
David's life was overshadowed with a dark, heavy cloud.
And he wept and cried bitterly very aloud.

"O my son. Absalom, my son, my son Absalom!
If only I had died instead of you!
O Absalom, my son, my son."

Absalom's death was like a venom and sting-
And David was in anguish more than any other King.
But were Absalom spared, he would have continued to fight-
And David would have been in a quandary and plight.

GOD'S HOUSE

2 SAMUEL 24: 1-25
1 CHRONICLES 21: 1-27

David ordered Joab to count all the people.
God view David's actions as most horrible.
Joab knew it was wrong, but complied anyway.
For the King over-ruled him and prevailed on that
Day.
The Lord disliked intensely, what David had done.
He sent a disease that brought the nation down.
Seventy thousand of them fell victim and died,
And those who survived it, lamented and cried.
A destroying angel targeted Jerusalem.
And the people it seemed, nothing could
Save them.
But God said to the angel, "Enough! Do no more."
As the angel was close to the treshing floor.
David was ordered to offer a sacrifice there.
And the site was earmarked for the house of
Prayer.
Araunah gave to David, the land free and clear
But the King didn't accept it, and paid what
Was fair.
It was where Isaac came close to being
Sacrificed.
But an angel stopped Abraham from plunging
His knife.
David offered his sacrifice there to the Lord.
And hoped that he and his master would be in one
Accord.

David said, "This is where the Lord's house will
Be built.
My neglect to do this has brought
Personal guilt.
Now the Lord God will have his
Own sacred space,
Where the King, priests and people, could
Seek out his face."

XXXX

PREPARING FOR GOD'S HOUSE

1 Kings 1: 1-53
1 Chronicles 22: 1-19

David had found a place to build the
Lord's house.
From his heart, he listened to God's inner
Voice.
God preferred to leave the building to
David's successor.
Because David, he said, was a warrior.
God wanted his house built by a man of peace,
And in Solomon's time, all warfare will cease.
David must put his great ambition on hold.
And do exactly as he was told.
David stored all the material for the house
Of God.
Everything was in place for the house of the Lord.
He told Soloman God promised him a reign
Of calm.
And he will build the Lord's house, when the time is
Calm.
When David grew old, Bathsheba came to him.
She reminded him of his promise, "Solomon would
Be King."
But Adonijah, she warned, was actively preparing
To make sure he would be the next Israelite King.
David promised Bathsheba her son would be enthroned.
The Kingship is his and not his brother's own.
"Today," he said, "I will make Solomon King."
Then Adonijah heard sounds of joyful singing.

The singing was resounding and it shook the
Ground.
And Adonijah was scared; he didn't want to
Stay around.
He was afraid that King Solomon would take
His life.
Because of his treason, and seditious strife.
But Solomon said to Adonijah, "You must
Go home.
Because as the King, I'm not picking a bone!"
He said to Adonijah, it was his choice to give.
And if he acts honorably, he will make him
Live.

XXXX

SAMSON & DELILAH

JUDGES CHAPTERS 13-16

The Angel told the woman of his birth long before.
And what she was hearing, she couldn't ignore.
She would give birth to a son, to be a Nazarite.
He would be strong, and deliver the Israelites.

He was one of the judges of Israel
Great stories of him I am going to tell.
A lion attacked him from the vineyard lowlands,
And he killed the creature with his two bare hands.

The name they had chosen for him, was Samson.
He was accused by the Philistines for acts of arson.
He caught three hundred foxes, and set their tails alight.
And released them in the standing grain to burn all night.

The Philistines responded by killing two of his own,
And in turn responded with a donkey's jawbone
He killed a thousand Philistines single handedly
And was known as the Philistines' arch enemy.

After Samson's wife death, he fell in love again,
To him, she was a very lovely dame.
She was known by the name, Delilah
And he hoped they'd be together forever.

Samson trusted Delilah, wholly and completely,
He didn't question at all her sincerity,
The Philistines' approached Delilah, with a plan and said,
"It's something you can carry out when he's preparing for bed."

"Find out what is the secret to his amazing strength,
You can surely find out if you're persistent."
Delilah was greatly tempted by the Philistines' offer:
The money she would get would increase her coffer.

So she kept asking Samson, the reason for his great strength.
But Samson would always tell her stories that he invent.
She kept probing and probing to get at the truth,
She had had enough of Samson's, persistent untruth.

Delilah, accused Samson, that he didn't love her,
Otherwise, he would have no problems with her to confer.
Samson listened carefully, and could no longer bear
So he told her the truth, "they must shave off my hair."

And when Samson was asleep, the Philistines came,
It was the moment of truth, and no longer a game,
They shaved off his hair while he was sound asleep,
And when he awoke, he was helplessly weak.

The Philistiens captured him, and gouged out his two eyes,
In spite of his moaning, groaning and cries.
They took him to prison, and he couldn't fight back,
He had suffered a significant and life-changing setback.

While Samson was in prison, he had time to reflect.
He was convinced that he was still the Lord's elect.
And he prayed to the Lord for his strength to regain,
And it did, as his hair started growing again.

As the Philistines worshiped their god, Dagon,
Large crowds were there and they brought out Samson,
They taunted and jeered, and made sport of him,
But Samson was praying to his God and King.

The Philistines assembled in an upstairs building.
Its pillars were strong and very imposing.
Samson brought down the building and it crashed to the ground.
He killed more Philistines, than in his whole life long.

Samson trusted Delilah, but she didn't love him.
She coaxed him and he told her everything.
It was an act of betrayal, that cost him his life,
By one close to him, like a trusted wife.

XXXX

SOLOMON PRAYS FOR WISDOM

1 Kings 3: 3-15

David was King of Israel for thirty three years.
When he died the people of Israel shed many tears.
And Solomon, as predicted to be King, was enthroned.
His Kingdom will be strong and have peace at home.

On the site where God's temple was to be built.
Solomon prayed and offered sacrifices for guilt.
One night, in a dream, when the air was quite still,
The Lord came and said to him, "Ask what you will."

He thoughtfully reflected on what the Lord said to him.
His choices must be right, being a very young king.
"Give me wisdom and knowledge, to know right from wrong."
He did not want to appear as being head strong.

Solomon, pleased the Lord, by asking for this.
For with such a request he wouldn't be amiss.
God said, "you didn't ask for your life to be long,
But you ask for those things that will make your reign strong."

"Nor did you ask for riches, victory and power
To wield it unwisely at any given hour!
Instead you asked for wisdom to judge my people.
To execute justice, as you are able."

God told him, "Because you didn't ask for the store."
He will give him abundantly and very much more.
"Yes, some other leaders will show insight, it's true.
But no other ruler will be compared with you."

"As long as you're faithful as your father David
Everything would be fine, wonderful and splendid."
The Lord will bless him with longevity.
And his reign will be marked by integrity.

XXXX

SHE WAS IMPRESSED

1 KINGS 10: 1-13

It was a journey she decided to undertake.
She must visit King Solomon at any rate.
The great things she had heard, she must prove them true.
So her visit was something that she had to do.

I speak of the beautiful Queen of Sheba.
Who lived in the distant South Arabia
The king was delighted and pleased to meet her,
The most beautiful queen from the land of Arabia.

She asked him difficult questions on many issues,
And Solomon had the answers for the ones she did chose,
She was impressed by his wisdom considerably,
And she exclaimed that, "The half has not been told me!"

She said the Lord who bestowed the kingship was blessed,
For his knowledge and wisdom had exceeded the best.
She presented to him treasures that made him wonder.
Then returned to her birthplace of Southern Arabia.

SOLOMON'S KINGDOM

1 KINGS 10:14-11:13

Solomon's elaborate buildings had a negative side;
They had to be maintained well, for his ego and pride.
He had to find the money, for his huge complexes,
So he imposed on the people very heavy taxes.

Some worked on the buildings as skilled carpenters.
Others defended the nation and became great soldiers.
Some worked in the fields and were servants for him.
And worked just like slaves for the insensitive King.

For he cared very little, for the poor of the land.
Something the God of Israel had to reprimand.
As he continued to stray and radically depart.
As if he didn't love the Lord God, with his whole heart.

His queen was the daughter of the Egyptian Pharaoh,
She did what she liked and he didn't say "no!"
She didn't submit at all to the God of Israel.
And caused religious confusion as the history will tell.

Solomon encouraged false gods near Jerusalem site,
Thus the future of Israel was not very bright.
He angered the Lord by this offensive thing,
And the Lord promised to take the Kingdom away from him,

"I would do it" God said, "after Solomon passed along,"
"Then I would rip the kingdom from the reign of his Son.
One tribe would be left as God's last final bid,
Because of the exemplary reign of his father David!

JEZEBEL

1 Kings 18: 16-40 I Kings 21: 1-24
II Kings 9: 32-37

I don't want to be like Jezebel,
Wife of Ahab, the King of Israel.
She was ruthless, heartless and a fearful woman,
Who was always involved in some devious plan.

I don't want to be like Jezebel.
She was deceitfully wicked, by no means an angel.
She accused and killed Naboth for his own piece of land.
What a notoriously evil, piece of firebrand!

I don't want to be like Jezebel.
She despised Elijah, after Mount Carmel.
Elijah proved that his God had the power to act
And that Baal, her god, had no life, that's a fact.

I don't want to be like Jezebel.
She was pushed out a high window, and to earth she fell.
She suffered bad injuries to her head.
And hungry dogs below made sure she was dead.

I don't want to be like Jezebel.
Dogs were waiting below at the time she fell.
They left only her skull, her feet and her hand
That was all they had left of this wicked woman.

So you see why I don't want to be like Jezebel.
She was the very incarnate of the Devil in Hell.
The dogs that devoured her ate like the dingo,
They consumed her in minutes, from head to toe.

XXXX

ZECHARIAH

LUKE CHAPTER 1

The Impossible became the Possible

Zechariah and his wife were both advanced in years.
They were faithful and dutiful in their religious affairs.
Both he and Elizabeth wanted to have a son,
But their age to them was like sterilization.

He was chosen as a priest, to burn incense at prayer,
At the altar, an angel appeared to him there.
Zachariah was afraid, and well shaken up.
And wondered for what purpose, he did interrupt!

The angel immediately put him at ease,
"Don't be afraid Zechariah, be at peace if you please.
Elizabeth, your wife is going to have a son,
It is sure to take place, it is God's decision."

"The first thing to note is, the child's name will be John.
He will proclaim the Lord Christ, till his work is done,
He will be the forerunner, for the coming of Christ,
He will urge them to listen, and take his advice."

Zechariah questioned the angel,. He didn't know what to do.
He asked, "How do I know what you're saying is true?
My wife and I are too old for a son!
If God wanted this to happen, he wouldn't have waited so long."

"I am Gabriel," he said, "messenger of the Lord.
He sent me in harmony, and not in discord.
But since you have chosen to doubt what is true.
Your mouth will be sealed till his word comes through."

From that moment, Zechariah couldn't utter a word,
But a large crowd outside could be noisily heard.
They asked, "why was Zechariah taking so long."
They concluded, "God Almighty had shut his mouth down."

Elizabeth became pregnant, as the angel said,
Soon there would be a baby boy to be put to bed.
Meanwhile, the matter re-surfaced, and was mentioned again,
What was to be chosen for the baby's name!

Choosing the wrong name, one could be awarded blame,
They said, "You can't name him John, it's not a family name."
The only way they had to resolve the matter
"Was to refer the decision to the muted father."

They gave him a pen and a writing slate,
The name he wrote down, none of them could relate.
"The child's name is John," that's what Zechariah wrote.
At that moment he spoke, and everyone took note.

Everyone who heard it, wondered about the boy,
Would he be at the altar, or God's vocal envoy?
John grew up as a preacher in the service of God.
Calling all to repentance for the coming of the Lord.

XXXX

THE CALL

MATTHEW 4:18-22

Jesus went walking by the Sea of Galilee
He saw Peter and Andrew whom he wanted to see,
They were fishing and casting a net into the sea,
Hoping for a catch, of some significant degree.

"Follow me!" Jesus said, "You must come and see!
I want you to join my new ministry.
You're going to change jobs; I'll be your Teacher and Friend.
I'll give you a new name, "the fishers of men."

They loved what they heard, Jesus called them to do.
They didn't question him, but believed it was true.
They left their nets forthwith, and followed him,
To be part of his ministry, a life-changing thing.

Further down, Jesus met also James and John
Who were fishing as brothers, united as one,
They were fishing with their father, named Zebedee,
They left him and joined Jesus immediately.

These men became the forefront of Christ's ministry.
Restoring men and women to spirituality.
Jesus wants you to be one of his disciples today.
To save some from becoming a castaway.

STOP THE FUNERAL

LUKE 7:11-16

Jesus and his disciples, went to a town called Nain,
And there another funeral was taking place again,
It wasn't an old man, or that of an aged wife,
It was a young man who was in the prime of his life.

A large crowd did follow the village gate
His mother also followed in a sorrowful state,
A widow she was with no one else to turn,
She was weeping and sobbing there all alone.

Jesus moved with pity, was compassionate,
And he stopped the procession, just outside the gate,
He went up to her and said, "Woman don't weep."
But her son was dead, and not merely asleep!

"I want to bring an end to this sad procession,"
Jesus said to the crowds with deep emotion.
"I can't bear to see this widow, cry out like this.
She needs some peace; not a crisis."

Jesus spoke this time, addressing the dead.
Some looked directly at the dead man's head.
"Young man," Jesus said, "I want you to get up."
And the young man awoke, right there on the spot.

When he got up, he also started to speak,
And surprisingly, his voice wasn't faint or weak.
Jesus took him and gave him back to his mother,
She embraced him, as though she would hold him forever.

The crowds were happy, but yet divinely afraid.
That a great prophet had come in their midst to their aid,
Jesus proved to them all without any question.
He was Lord of life, and the resurrection.

NICODEMUS

JOHN 3:

A ruler of the Jews went to Jesus by night,
He didn't want to be seen going there in day-light.
We know not the month, whether May or August.
But we know the man's name was Nicodemus.

He said, "Jesus we know you're one sent from God.
Your works and your deeds are in one accord.
You're truly the one who is Godly and true;
For no one can do the great works that you do."

It was a teaching moment for his mouth to open,
And he told Nicodemus about the kingdom of heaven.
For a person to enter God's kingdom and reign,
He must live in the Spirit and be born again.

Nicodemus said to him, "Tell me, how could this be?
For an adult grown person to be born anew?
Could he enter the womb again and be born?
This is confusing to me, whether night-time or dawn."

Jesus said, "You must be born of water and the spirit.
And you should not marvel as I have made mention of it.
If eternal life is what you're seeking to gain.
I told you once more, you must be born again."

St.John tells us in chapter three and verse sixteen.
What God did in Christ, for all human beings
For God gave his Son Jesus, who paid the full price,
That all might benefit from eternal life.

A MAN BORN BLIND

ST. JOHN CHAPTER 9

An unnamed man was born most unfortunate,
From the day of his birth, blindness was his fate
He hope that one day someone would find the key,
To open his eyes so that he could see.

He heard about Jesus, the Messiah, and King,
Who had the power to reverse almost anything.
And one day, Jesus had fortunately passed by,
So he thought it worth while, to give it a try.

Some questioned the reason, why he was born blind.
And his parents, and his sins did come to mind.
Jesus said, he was born blind so the works of God,
Would be made manifest, locally and abroad.

Jesus said, "Tell me sir, how can I help you?
He replied, "Lord you know I really would like to see!"
Jesus spat on the ground and made it into mud.
He was about to nip the blindness in the bud.

He rubbed some of the mud over the man's eyes.
And after washing, he looked up and saw the skies.
And after so many years living in obscurity,
"At long last," he said," I am able to see.

The Jews couldn't believe that it was the same man.
"How now he can see!" They couldn't understand.
"Who opened your eyes?" they asked inquiringly.
"You're not the same man who stands here and can see!"

"A man named Jesus, put mud on my eyes.
And now I can see the white clouds and blue skies.
He must be a prophet to do such great work,
To help someone like me, a poor helpless folk."

The Jews went to his parents, to get at the truth.
And they heard the same story; nothing different to hoot.
What the-once-blind-man said, was the fact of the case.
They vouched "he was blind at this very birth place."

His parents said, "This is our son, we know that for sure.
He was born blind, I can't tell you any more.
We wish we can tell you who opened his eyes.
Ask him, he'll confirm the truth from the lies!"

The man couldn't bear their interrogation any more,
He was ready at any moment to show them the door,
He took the time to tell them with bold certainty,
That "whereas I was blind, now I see!"

The Jews put him out of their worship that day
They felt he had too many good things about Jesus to say.
But what ever they did, he was very forthright.
Because he knew it was Jesus, who gave him his sight.

Jesus posed a question, as a sounding board.
And asked him if he did believe in the Lord.
He said, "Who is he sir? That I might believe in him now."
Jesus said, "I am he," and he did worship and bow.

XXXX

THE DEATH AND RESURRECTION OF OUR LORD JESUS CHRIST

By Augustine Joseph
(Poet of Merit International Society of Poets)

His Hour came; He said to them,
"I must visit Jerusalem,"
The donkey that He rode upon,
Heard the "Hosannas" people sang.

The crowds ahead, like those behind;
Sang jubilantly all the time,
They spread palm branches in the way,
"Blessed is He," they sang that Day.

The Jewish meal, called Passover,
Jesus ate as the Last Supper,
Eleven disciples shocked, you see,
Heard: "One of you will betray me."

Just as He said, Judas came forth,
And kissed the Lord, to have him caught,
False charges brought; truth at a loss,
Nothing will save Him from the Cross.

The soldiers grabbed him; stripped him bare;
Gave Him a scarlet robe to wear,
They made a crown of thorns instead,
And placed it firmly on His head.

With taunting, mockeries and jeers,
They hurled insults close to his ears
A weighty cross they gave to Him,
The price He paid for our sin.

On Calvary they nailed Him fast,
Secured him on the Cross at last,
From there He gave the "Seven Words,"
Before his fading eyes were closed.

O yes, they thought it was the end,
But a new life returned again,
Three days had passed since His last breadth,
The Lord Jesus had conquered death
Two Marys expecting the worst,
Went to the tomb, and saw him first;
In disbelief at what they saw,
Awestruck! Dumbfounded even more.
He called the Eleven to regroup;
The word must go outside the loop.
"Spread the Good News; nations to reach,
I am with you, Baptize and teach."

WHY THE RESURRECTION?

Jesus, the Messiah came into this world,
His birth and his death were already foretold,
The Pharisees, to him, were a spiritual albertros,
They arrested him and crucified him on the cross.

Joseph buried his body in his own grave,
Jesus, the Lord who had come to save,
Joseph wondered, if his hopes would all be in vain,
Or whether he would see his Lord, Jesus again.

But on the third day, he was no where among the dead,
And had abandoned the wrapping attached to his head.
He rose from the dead, leaving the grave behind,
In triumph as the Lord of all humankind.

The Resurrection took place, not for Christ's personal gain,
It took place for us to spiritually attain,
Eternal life in the kingdom of heaven,
And after death, we too, new life will be given.

When he rose from the dead, he had conquered sin,
And he showed himself first, to Mary Magdalene.
She must go and tell the others, that he is alive
And what he had said before, had to materialize.

The Resurrection took place, not for Christ's personal gain,
It took place, for us to conquer sin and reign.
Attain Eternal life, in the kingdom of heaven,
As the door that was closed, is now widely open.

When Jesus Christ rose, he could have gone straight to heaven,
But he chose to reveal himself to the eleven.
Jesus passed on his peace, and gave them their mission.
They must forgive sins, and give absolution.

When he rose, there was one that he couldn't bypass.
So he went and reached out to doubting Thomas.
Jesus called him to touch the marks of the nails.
He must see for himself, and share the details.

FROM DOUBTER TO BELIEVER

DOUBTING THOMAS: FROM DOUBTER TO BELIEVER
ST. JOHN 20: 19-30

You must meet this man we all talk about.
There was hardly anyone stronger in his doubt,
His fellow disciples came to him with the news
But Thomas won't believe, he just simply refused.

Jesus had appeared, and greeted most of them.
But Thomas wasn't there with the other men.
So they broke the good news to him the next day.
But Thomas still doubted and insisted, "no way!"

Joyfully, they told him, "We have seen the Lord!"
He had previously appeared and addressed them all.
But Thomas thought the whole thing incredulous,
And he began to question, their level of trust.

He described the yard stick for him to believe.
What they told him was too much to conceive.
"Unless I could see the marks of the nail
Anything else is like a fairy tale."

Jesus later appeared when Thomas was there,
He said, "Thomas, get up, put your finger here.
You wanted to see the wound in my side.
Come closer, look here: see how deep and wide."

Thomas was dumb-founded and totally in awe,
No longer the same man as he was before,
He fell on his knees, saying, "my Lord and God!"
Ready to proclaim the "Goodness of the Lord."

You too might be doubtful of God in your life.
Like some unsure surgeon with his surgery knife.
"Believe in the Lord, what ever you do.
Doubt not, and fear not, for his word is true."

XXXX

THE NAMELESS PROCLAIMED HIS NAME

ACTS CHAPT. 3

He was nameless and sat at the Beautiful
Gate.
A cripple who saw no change in his state.
So daily he sat begging alms to get by,
Not expecting any help from on high.

Both Peter and John at the hour of prayer,
Met the crippled man who was sitting there.
He extended his hands to receive some money.
But Peter and John saw an opportunity.

"Look at us!" said Peter the apostle, to him.
The cripple was still expecting something.
"Silver and gold have I none." Peter said
I have something better for you instead."

"In the name of Jesus, I want you to walk,
You'll see action and not just talk."
And Peter grasped his right hand, and he stood
Up to walk.
And all were amazed at the miracle wrought.

Many crowds were attracted by what had been done.
To Solomon's Portico the people did run!
Peter explained to them, the whole truth of the
Case.
"It was Jesus who made him walk by his grace."

"The people," he said, "shouldn't be surprised at all."
It wasn't their own deed, but Jesus their Lord.
The same Jesus they tried and condemned to death.
Will perform many more wonders, they haven't seen yet.

Pilate said, he would release him, the
Innocent one,
But they insisted, that their will be done.
And God in his power, raised him up from
The dead.
Now He is the church's Power, Authority and
Head.
"This man who sat daily at this Beautiful
Gate.
Was not destined to live in a hopeless state.
We are witnesses here to what we see unfold.
It was Jesus by which this man was made
Whole."

XXXX

PENTECOST

ACTS Chapter 2

They came, assembled one and all,
The Day the Spirit on them fall,
Early they sat; long before noon,
Expectant in the dormant room;

Then suddenly with a mighty power,
The Spirit came and took over,
A wind-like force on them from heaven,
Announced the Holy Ghost was given.

And each one there was spirit-filled,
Just as the Lord in Joel willed,
With unknown tongue each one did speak,
No voice was timid, faint or weak.

Each one proclaimed God's mighty deed,
With messages the people need,
Onlookers there were mesmerized,
By what they saw, and criticized.

"These men are drunk, and still want more!
Some slept at the ABC door."
But Peter set the record straight,
Told them God's word he would translate.

God's promised Holy Ghost was given,
That's why the Spirit came from heaven,
The Apostles on their mission went,
Reason why Paul gave up his tent;

The Spirit sent them to and fro;
To Asia Minor they would go,
God's message of salvation told,
It must go out to all the world.

The Spirit seeks after the lost,
Like Jesus Christ on Calvary's Cross.
"Come Holy Ghost, our souls inspire."
Help us to catch the Spirit's "fire."

ANANIAS & SAPPHIRA

ACTS 5: 1-11

Ananias and Sapphira were husband and wife,
And both of them wanted an abundant life.
So they conspired to cheat about the price they received.
For property sold, they both planned to deceive

The church was expanding greatly at the time.
Others sold their possessions, withheld not a dime!
The money was given to the Church for its work,
To spread the Gospel of Christ, both to near and far folk.

For example, Joseph also known by the name Barnabas,
Gave the money from a sale, he wasn't like Judas!
There he laid every cent at the apostle's feet,
And then left for home, by way of the street.

Everyone had enough, no one was in need,
The spirit of generosity discouraged any greed.
The church reached out in service to everyone.
It was said, they all," Had everything in common."

But Ananias and Sapphira sold their plot of land.
Ananias came first, maybe being the man.
He gave part of the proceeds as being the full price.
And felt everything was acceptable, dandy and nice.

Peter said," Why did you lie to the Holy Spirit?"
And he fell down and died there for doing it.
Sapphira came by later, after a three-hour wait.
And she too sadly came to a similar fate.

XXXX

CORNELIUS & PETER

ACTS CHAP. 10

A centurion, named Cornelius in the Italian cohort
We know not the battles, he actually fought.
He lived at the Time in Caesarea
And was directed to visit the apostle, Peter.

He was a generous and very religious man.
Who gave cheerfully to his fellow man
His devotion to God was in regular prayer.
To gain spiritual strength to persevere.

It was about three in the evening, while he was at prayer
An angel's visit in a vision was clear.
"Cornelius," he said, "You have found favor with God.
Your prayers have reached up to the ears of the Lord."

The angel told him, he must meet with Peter.
Who lived at the time in a place called Joppa
Peter, who was also known by the name of Simon,
They both shared in God's mission and exaltation.

Cornelius sent a party to meet with Peter.
To see how both of them could work together
Meanwhile, Peter went up on the house top to pray.
From there he would know what the Lord had to say.

In a vision, he saw something like a great sheet.
Lowered from the four corners of the earth to his feet.
In it were all kinds of creatures as potential meat.
Urging Peter to rise, to "kill and eat."

Peter said, "Nothing common or unclean, O Lord,
Has passed my lips, it's a true record."
The Lord told him, "Call nothing common or unclean.
What God has purified, for all human beings."

While Peter contemplated, the meaning of the dream.
He was about to know more, about the vision he had seen.
With Cornelius' party arrival at the door.
He couldn't ignore the Gentiles anymore!

FAITH

What is this virtue known as
Faith?
Get it from God, and do not wait.
A state of strong conviction hold.
Believe, though evidence not told.

It calls for deep belief in God
Unshaken firmly in the Lord.
But oh how hard when it comes
The test
The faith we must display the best.

A person terminal in pain,
We pray and pray and pray
Again.
Regardless of the end in view.
The faith they have will see them
Through.

Faith sometimes like a mustard
Seed.
Have great effect to show God's deed.
What ever problem big or long,
If mountainous, faith brings it down.

David, faced with Goliath's
Wrath.
He had faith in God, the only path.
His size was small, his faith
Was strong.
And soon Goliath was on the ground.

Jesus did nothing without faith
Provide the food, the hungry ate.
He made the sick get out of bed
And called Lazarus from the dead.

Without faith, we can never please
God.
We do it in the name of the Lord.
Apply your faith and see it's true
What God enables you to do.

XXXX

PRAYER

St. Luke 11: 1-13
James 5: 13-18
1 Kings 3: 5-14

Jesus says "ask, and it will be given unto you."
Call on his name, and he'll prove that it's true.
He says "seek" and we'll certainly find,
That God is caring, generous and kind.
In addition he says to persistently knock,
Calling on God is never magic or luck!
It's something we must do faithfully every day,
Persistency is required often when we pray.
God answers prayers consistent with his will.
In that way his purposes we are sure to fulfill.
Jesus taught us this truth, in what we call "The Lord's Prayer"
We do as he says, and gains a listening ear.
James writes about the prayer of the righteous man.
To him, God gives power as we know that he can.
And the sick man or woman will get out of bed;
No longer enfeebled, but stronger instead!
Prayer is asking God which direction to go.
Without it we are confused from our head to toe,
Young Solomon prayed, when he ascended the throne,
I wish people would pray as they use their cell phone.
Young King Solomon, did have the knack of prayer.
And God listened to him with an attentive ear.
He asked for wisdom and an understanding heart;

To govern and lead his people from the very start;
God says, if we humble ourselves and pray,
And turn away from our sins each and every day
He will forgive over and above seven times seven;
And will hear our prayer from his throne in heaven.

XXXXXXXXX

THE NETWORKS

SEPTEMBER 20, 2000

Competing for the news each day,
Each network wants the first say:
"We have some breaking news to tell
No other network does it as well.

"An incident, that is news-worthy,
We must be there!" says ABC.
"The people need the truth to know.
First ABC to the site must go."

"A news report in Italy
Must be covered," says NBC.
"We'll send reporters to the spot.
Right where the news is breaking hot!"

"We are like vultures of the news,
And CBS, nothing refuse!
We'll tell it with a little spin
To make our story great, and win."

"We'll cover stories anywhere.
No news if CNN's not there!
We'll traverse over earth and sky
To ask the questions Who? and Why?

And when elections come along,
They say they do not care who's won.
But make predictions loud and clear—
The first with it over the air.

"THE NETWORKS"

Competing for the news each day
Each network wants the first to say:
"We have a breaking news to tell.
No other newscast does it well."

An incident happened of some degree
'We must be there!" said ABC
"The people need the facts you know."
"So to the site our news team go."

A news report comes from Italy,
"We must cover it," says NBC.
"We'll send reporters to the spot.
"Right where the news is breaking hot."

"We're the vultures of the news!
And CBS nothing refuse!
We may tell it with a little spin.
To make our story great and win."

"We'll cover stories anywhere!
No news, if CNN not there.
We'll traverse over sea and sky
To ask the questions, what? And why?"

"We at FOX keep a low profile,
We have a very different style.
We'll try to bring you all the news
And Know, we are the ones you'll choose."

DOUBT

The thing is there for you to claim.
But doubt enters your mind again;
You always feel the best is due,
To someone else but not for you.

Your mind told you, what you should be
An open opportunity.
But all your hopes will be in vain,
As doubt enters your mind again.

And so you put the thought on hold,
An idea hot has now gone cold
For doubt has done its job once more
And robs you empty; leaves you poor.

It's in your heart to teach a class,
To share your knowledge there at last,
But doubt tells you, "It can't be done!
Give up and don't attempt this one."

And so you cast aside your goal
"In future years it will unfold."
But know this truth, you'll not attain,
Since you let doubt control your brain.

SPIN ANCHOR

(1) I'm sometimes very greatly amused,
How some news-anchor do bring the news.
If it is something that they support
They spin till it reaches center court.
But if it is something they really hate,
They spin to make everyone irate.

Refrain
All they should do is just tell the news,
Without giving any of their personal views,
Because most of the people are smart enough
So anchor, leave out all of your bias stuff.

(2) Just take a look at the Anchor's face,
It tells you they have already decided the case,
When news break out 'that's in their favor,
Glee on their faces beaming all over
But if it is news, they didn't like that night
They present it to all, in the worst of light.

All they should do is just tell the news,
Without giving any of their personal views,
Because most of the people are smart enough
So Anchor, leave out all of your personal stuff.

(3) They make use of certain emotive words.
To hide the real news with spin overloads.
They learn the culture of spin so well
To boost and help their ratings to swell
Don't give me news with any pork belly-
Just give the facts; leave the rest to me.

XXXX

THE IMPORTANCE OF SELF-ESTEEM

(1) I often wonder what's better than a good self-esteem.
It's integral to one's life as a human being.
A positive self image is worth more than gold.
It prepares one for life over a thousand fold.

(2) It's a sense of feeling good about oneself.
And to face unforeseen challenges of life itself.
It's a feeling of success and competence,
And to approach situations with confidence.

(3) Let no one make you think, you aren't worth anything.
That's because they're envious and act intimidating.
Remember God made you special with amazing value.
So don't listen to those who tell you that it isn't true.

(4) Love is important in having a good self-esteem.
Not being judgmental when one has to intervene
It's having an awareness of oneself and one's right
And would defend it anytime, whether day or night.

(5) Self-esteem is an awareness to keep healthy and strong.
It helps you to know when one is engaged in wrong.
Self-esteem is important like fish is to water,
We couldn't live with out it if life is to be any better.

(6) Self-esteem does not embarrass a child or a kid
That's inviting the thing of which we want to get rid,
We should encourage the child for his success and skill,
And he will do even better with more practice and drill.

(7) Self-esteem thinks no less of anyone else,
Nor thinks one is inferior or better than oneself.
But it will persue one's goal as a thing to achieve,
For that is what a good self-esteem truly believe.

(8) Building a good self-esteem is not automatic,
You have to work hard at it and be systematic,
And your child will turn out close to perfection,
And he would have achieved the best thing next to salvation.

XXXX

MANY THINGS THAT WE DO NOT KNOW

(1) We know that the human being, has an intelligent brain
And that the mind thinks up thoughts like a gushing fountain.
Yet even when it is working to over-flow,
There are still many things that we do not know.

(2) We have studied the brain cells, and know how they work.
We know the signs and conditions of an imminent stroke.
We have studied and know what gives good-blood-flow,
But there are many things that we still do not know.

(3) We are smart and intelligent about many things,
We know all the US presidents, and British Kings.
We may answer all the questions on the jeopardy show,
But there are many things that we do not know.

(4) We know a great deal about plant and animal life,
We know Queen Jezzebel was King Ahab's wife.
We know carbon dioxide causes plants to grow
But there are many other things that we do not know.

(5) We are versed in the period of the dinosaurs.
We know the events that led up to the two World Wars;
We know that one can not stand straight, without one's little toe;
But there are other things we do not know.

(6) We know the world is the work of the Creator,
It was not caused by a big bang or an inventor.
We know why at sunset the sun sinks very low,
But there are many other things that we do not know.

(7) We know what causes the airplane to fly in the sky,
And why the bumble bee tries, but still can not fly.
We know of the brilliant writer, Edgar Allen Poe,
But there are many things that we do not know.

(8) We know who caused the destruction on 9/11.
And why God fearing people will go to heaven,
We know that Osama Bin Laden, was reported as dead
And was buried at sea, after the Koran was read.

(9) We know what causes a recession and a bad economy,
We know what is necessary to run the whole country,
We know why some politicians conveniently vote "no."
But there are many other things that we do not know.

(10) We know Jesus is the Savior of the world,
And He is calling each one to be part of his fold;
For to heaven the faithful ones will go
This important truth, some still do not know!

(11) Farm-workers supply our food-crops year by year;
But they have issues of which most are aware.
Your donations could ease what they undergo.
This is one thing that many people don't know.

(12) Dr. Eric Williams, a great leader of Trinidad and Tobago,
Wrote the historic book: "From Columbus to Castro."
And Barbados could boast of Mr. Errol Barrow,
But there are many other things that we do not know.

(13) We know President Obama is born citizen of the Unites States.
  And the computer Master-mind is Mr. Bill Gates;
  We know prisoners of conscience cry out: "Let Us Go!"
  Over 300,000 of them, world-wide you should know.

(14) We know that Prince William got married to Kate Middleton,
  In West Minister Abbey in the city of London.
  We know that two billion viewed it on the TV show.
  Would Prince Harry be next? We really don't know!

(15) We know that Barbados is known as "Little Britain,"
  It's the most English Island in the Caribbean.
  We know that its greatest leader was Mr.Errol Barrow,
  But there are many other things that we do not know.

(16) We know that highway accidents claim two lives every hour,
  And more die from suicide, than in conflicts of war.
  WE know that land mines inflict daily, a terrible death-blow.
  But there are many other things that we do not know.

(17) WE know that 800 million go hungry world-wide everyday.
  And 44 million child laborers in India fall prey.
  We know our world still have slaves, 27 million or so,
  But there are many other things that we do not know.

XXXX

"THE INCREDIBLE DREAM"

I was having an incredible dream one night.
Two men were talking about their first flight.
One said, "it's an outrage and couldn't be right."
It was Orville, the brother of Wibur Wright.

"We two brothers are hurt by 9/11.
We didn't know this was what was going to happen.
If we knew, we should really be called insane,
For our invention known as the aeroplane."

"America, I want you to know we are sorry
What happened to the nation on 9/11.
Were it not for the planes, there'd be no such horrors.
That killed so many people in the Twin Towers."

Wilbur said, "WE thought that we were doing some good.
In the interest of world-wide brother hood.
But some misused and abused our great invention.
And crated a scene of total mayhem."

I said, "Guys don't feel guilty at all about that.
You're not blame-worthy, and caused the attack.
Don't carry this load by taking the blame,
Every nation on earth loves the aeroplane."

SHARE THE DREAM

BY THE REV. AUGUSTINE JOSEPH

"I have a dream to share with you,
For you to share with others too.
America needs a racial bond,
For the United States to live as one."

"I gave my life in fighting hate.
My voice was heard in every State.
I planned to fight till victory's won,
My watchword: "We Shall Overcome!""

"I promulgated harmony,
That peoples everywhere be free,
I pledged to make the U.S. one,
Sing with me, "We Shall Overcome!""

"My words spoken with eloquence,
I urged, "Remove the racial fence!
They sought my life, I had to run,
While singing, "We Shall Overcome!""

"they set fierce dogs with snarling teeth,
To maul me from myl head to feet,
Attacks, bloody, vicious and long,
I never ceased to sing my song."

"Experienced life both down and up,
My gaze fixed on the Mountain top.
Propelled before the enemy's gun,
"Oh yes, I know we'll overcome!"

"One sad day in a balcony,
A bullet dropped me to my knee,
I whispered low, 'My work isn't done!"
With God, one day, we'll overcome!"

A GRAVE COMPLAINT

Cigarrettes Caused My Demise
By Augustine Joseph

I was taking a walk, just the other day,
When distinctly I heard a weird voice say,
"You're to blame for bringing me here,
Now that I'm dead, you really don't care."
I looked around, but I saw no one,
At first, a thought came to me to run,
The voice came out of a cemetery,
And it aroused my fearful curiosity.

On a graveside nearby, was a cigarette end
The voice said, "You caused my life to expend.
You told me to smoke about three packs a day,
Now here I am, all my bones decay."
The cigarette said, "You let a trash like me!
Bring you here in this cemetery?
Those who don't smoke, they are very wise,
They don't follow me to cause their demise."

But the voice repeated its sad refrain,
And blamed the cigarette once again,
"You told me that smoking, is really cool,
Now I am dead, too late, I'm the fool."

THE CRAZIEST SECONDS IN NORTH CAROLINA

(1) They ripped through the county of Cumberland,
With power and force in total command.
Eighty five people wounded, and at least one person dead,
Tornadoes bore down, causing panic and dread.

(2) It was the 16th of April, 2011,
The clouds at a sudden began to darken,
No one predicted the danger that lay ahead,
And the damage to the state would be so widespread.

(3) Three others were killed in Bladen County,
and one person in Dunn added to the tragedy.
It was a violent system from across the Midwest,
That put North Carolina through an acid test.

(4) In Cumberland County strong winds left their mark,
They overturned vehicles in the streets and the park.
The damage spanned a distance between eight to ten miles,
You knew you were in danger by the angry skies.

(5) From North Riley Road, to North Ramsey Street,
In some lively neighborhood, destruction was complete,
It was necessary for the city as well as the county.
To declare and enforce a state of emergency.

(6) People warned often about affected areas,
Because of fallen trees and some live wires,
Both LaGrange and Summerhill off North Riley Road,
Were hit hard, including Cottonade off Yadkin Road.

(7) The story was the same in College Lakes near Ramsey Street,
And Breakwater Bridge Road within the Beaver Dam's reach.
The tornadoes touched down ominously at about four.
As though they came for two things, to break down and devour.

(8) They snapped trees in half, and ripped some out of the ground.
While some neighborhoods were flattened like a playground,
Many people in shock, walked aimlessly around,
they had never seen tornadic winds ever so strong!

(9) So they had to watch out for down power lines,
Still deadly to take any unsuspecting lives.
The scenes were chaotic, all over the place,
Some struggled to emerge from any open space.

(10) A business man said, he saw his roof blow away,
His name was given as one Michael Ray.
He was grateful that his customers were safely inside
Together they cuddled, and cower and hide.

(11) Meanwhile, young business man Choe, gave thanks for his son,
Who helped save his life when the assault began.
They both stood at the counter when they saw the twister,
But his son, pulled him down quickly, and escaped the danger.

(12) The scene wasn't much different on North Riley Road,
When the tornadoes power began to unload.
People sought shelter in the Farmer's Market bathroom.
They thought things spelled nothing but gloom and doom.

(13) The roof of the bathroom flew off in a flesh.
They decided against making an uncertain dash,
The young kids in the group had fear in their eyes.
When they looked up and saw the open skies.

(14) Merciless and ruthless they took the low road.
And destroyed the True Vine Ministries on North Riley Road.
The people in the building heard the bombshell,
As one person was injured as the wall fell.

(15) Meanwhile, some were transported for medical attention.
Others taken to Dunn to Betsy Johnson.
Some went to the hospital all on their own,
To check out the extent of injuries unknown.

(16) Three emergency shelters became the instant abode,
One was Seventy First high School on Raeford Road.
The Spring Lake middle School was also a life-saver,
While the other was Westover Recreation Center.

(17) Andrews and McArthur Roads were in jeopardy,
Including Good Year Tire & Rubber Company.
Areas near Pine Forest High School didn't fare very well,
And the houses around, where some people dwell.

(18) the tornadoes ripped through town-houses and apartments,
Like a war-zone the sounds heard, were like bombardments.
A man said, "It's the craziest thing I have ever seen"
You could tell by the sound of the victim's scream.

(19) He said, a wall of his apartment blew a distant apart.
A piece of glass in the wall stuck there like a dart.
The force of the tornadoes was indescribable'
We were facing a power that was invincible.

(20) Places in Dunn and Wilson and North Raleigh,
  Were battered and destroyed significantly
  Each place had it's own gruesome story to tell,
  Of the raging tornadoes no one could quell.

(21) Four children were killed in Stony Brook Complex,
  In Raleigh some people were dazed and perplexed,
  As four very young lives were just snatched away,
  And all they could do, was cry out loudly and pray.

(22) In Sanford, the Lowe's roof was also blown away,
  But the manager's quick thinking did save the day!
  He told the workers, seek shelter quickly in the back,
  And saved employee's lives from the tornadoes attack.

(23) Twenty four people to date sadly lost their lives.
  We're touched, especially, when a little child dies.
  Some families will never forget that awful day.
  In which their loved ones were suddenly taken away!

(24) Governor Purdue made a passionate appeal for the cause,
  A dire situation like this will give anyone pause.
  She needed help for the victims left homeless and in need,
  There comes a joyful feeling in doing a very good deed.

(25) The estimate of the damage was mind-bogling.
  The sights left behind, were too devastating.
  No one wants to see ever these killers again,
  They are repugnantly repulsive, and have our disdain.

A GREYHOUND DRIVER

Some are serious; others jovial and kind.
Some information-driven, others disincline.
Some are silent and quiet, just like the night.
They'd point out not even, a historic site.

Some are humorous, and make passengers laugh,
Like one from Cheyenne, who was up to the task.
He tells of a driver St. Peter reinstate.
And edged out two Bishops at heaven's gate.

The bishops asked St. Peter, the question "why?"
He left them at the gate as two stand by!
"For as bishops, we preached to some great masses.
Out-numbering, all of the Greyhounds full buses."

But St. Peter said, "O bishops, that is really true,
There's one thing in your preaching, you didn't do.
You didn't scare the congregations to turn to the Lord,
To sing his praises with one accord."

"But the Greyhound driver, in the way that he drove
Scared the passengers all as he grazed the mangrove.
And scared "the Hell out of everyone,
Something, I wish you two bishops had done."

So that is why you bishops are not going through.
We need some fiery and scary sermons too.
People seldom take action to avoid a scare.
They must see Hell as something, worse than a nightmare.

THE LORD DID IT!

By Augustine Joseph, Poet of Merit Award
(International Society of Poets)

She spoke about Katrina's rage.
The high water at every stage,
She struggled up a hill a bit,
Reach safer ground, the Lord did it!

Others thankfully, dodged the deadly dome,
It held more danger than their home,
Katrina gave them all a fit,
They made it through, the Lord did it!

You too have stories, weird to tell,
To enchant us as casting a spell,
You too I'm sure escaped the pit,
You know for sure, the Lord did it.

A mother fought life all alone.
to feed the mouths of eight at home;
Tired, but stole some time to sit,
She thanked the Lord for doing it!

A man wanted to feed the poor,
He prayed to God: "Open a door."
He won a million dollars ticket,
"Alleluia!", he said, "The Lord did it!".

You ask me how I'm standing here!
After an accident so severe!
"No broken bones; no broken hip,
I'm telling you, the Lord did it."

All of you lifted me in prayer,
Your faith taught you the Lord would hear
Your prayers like candles brightly lit,
We shout once more, THE LORD DID IT!

FROM MANNA TO MANAGEMENT

(1) If I were a director, I would put it on the screen.
The history of the Jews, is one that should be seen.
Throughout their history, they had to circumvent
To move up from manna, to management.

(2) Many road-blocks and setbacks were put in their way
But they kept their belief in God, strong everyday.
Their faith was their bedrock for them to stand on,
For they knew that they had the tetragrammaton.

(3) It began with the patriarch, Abraham
God called him from Ur of the Chaldean.
He was accustomed to do things his own pace,
But God called, and told him, to: "Leave this place."

(4) God promised to make his whole family great.
Blessings, for his offsprings, an enormous estate.
But Abraham was puzzled, he didn't comprehend,
Because up to that time, he had no children.

(5) God took him outside to look up at the stars.
Among them was even the planet, Mars.
God asked him to see, if he could really count them.
For as many will be his future generation.

(6) God blessed him, and Sarah with Isaac, their son.
And from there, the growth of the people began.
Tension developed between, his wife known as Sarah,
And his concubine, bearing the name of Hagar.

(7) Pharaoh invited Joseph, down from Egypt's land
   He love it, and thought the River Nile was grand.
He persuaded his brother to come down and live there,
   There was plenty of food, and enough to spare.

(8) So the people of Israel settled down in Egypt,
As their populations increased, the Egyptians didn't like it.
Meanwhile, King Pharaoh came up with his own solution,
   To oppress, and enslave the Hebrew population.

(9) Of his great building projects, the nation took note,
   He forced all the Hebrews to go out to work.
But those who refused and didn't go willingly
   Were beaten and whipped continually.

(10) By then, Moses was born and saw the harsh condition.
   God called him to work for their liberation.
he went to King Pharaoh, whom he did not know.
   And told him God said, "let my people go!"

(11) Pharaoh, agreed, but soon he changed his mind,
And God brought plagues on Egypt from time to time.
   Finally, God sent Moses with the usual refrain.
And Moses told Pharaoh, "You won't see me again!"

(12) God told Moses get ready to leave Egypt's land
   It wasn't a joke, it was God's urgent command.
The Hebrews were ready and headed for the Red Sea.
   They were on their way to be happy and free!

(13) The Egyptians tried to reach them, to bring them back,
   But it wasn't happening: and that was a fact.
The waters parted and the Hebrews went through.
   The Egyptians followed, but didn't know what to do.

(14) The waters came back rushing mightily,
And all the Egyptians, were drowned in the sea.
The Israelites were happy and gave thanks to God
For saving them from Pharaoh, the Egyptian overlord.

(15) The Hebrews spent a long time in the wilderness.
Moses tried to lead them; they had a problem with this!
They complained about food, and were hunger-driven,
And God gave them manna, he sent from heaven.

(16) And who could forget the Maccabean revolt?
When the Syrians attack was like a violent jolt?
But Judas Maccabeas fought back very hard
And hammered the enemy out of their backyard.

(17) And what about the Masada, and the holocaust?
Devastating events of the distant past!
Now the Jews are watchful, these don't happen again.
For they left their mark, and indelible pain!

(18) Fast forward to the Jews in America
They have control of Wall Street and the US dollar.
They're making a statement of acknowledgment,
That they have moved up from manna to management.

DRESSING UP FOR THE JURY

I know a young man, whose last name is Sands,
His baggy pants falling, and grabbed by both hands.
One day I saw him, dressed up like a groom.
I didn't know he was headed for the court room.

Oh how I pray that our young men would dress!
Handsomely clad, and looking their best!
Why leave the finest suit for the court?
As if going to a conference of great import.

It is clear that this young man do have decent clothes,
Why not wear them elsewhere, God alone knows.
He should step out very proudly, and uplift his race,
And never for one moment try to be a disgrace.

It is time that our young men show some ambition.
Not dressing for the courthouses all over the land.
So get in the habit to always look your best,
Choosing the right clothes on the way to success.

Don't miss the one point that I'm making here.
Dressing only for the courts, we have to repair
Walk not the streets with trousers at the knees,
Dress well, O young man, I'm begging you please.

COMPUTER PLAGIARISM

1. With the coming of the computer on the world scene,
    A language it stole came with it into being.
    I wish it would leave our English words alone,
    And come up with a language all of its own!
2. "Browse" doesn't mean what it used to mean,
    It is something you do on the display screen.
    A mouse was a rodent in a house or lab,
    Now it's a hand-held device oval like a pad.
3. A virus was a fearful and dreaded disease,
    Now it's an interference that does as it please,
    A window used to bring light and air indoors,
    Now it's a computer method to be explored
4. "Scroll" is no more a piece of manuscript;
    A "Conference Room" has no chairs in it!
    "Roadrunner was a very quick-running bird,
    Now it's a program to help the user download.
5. A friend of mine was referring to a special menu,
    I thought he meant a tasty Jamaican stew.
    But he said, "No. I meant a computer word,
    So I said to him, you're being absurd!
6. "Surfing" was done only out at sea,
    Now students surf in their dormitory,
    They grab the mouse; click on the World Wide Web,
    Now the spider has to say it's weaving its thread.
7. And most of them speak of a megabyte,
    And McDonald Big Mack, I think of, alright!
    Computer jargon has really taken hold,
    It's everywhere now, throughout the whole world.

MY SPECIAL VALENTINE

There couldn't be a better time,
To speak of my dear Valentine.
To tell you how much I do care.
Yes, sweetheart, no one else compare.

Oft I would call you my baby,
It tells of the love I have for you.
When first we met at school, in class.
I knew for certain it would last.

My love extends, yes, far and wide.
Embraces you close to my side.
The time spent together as two good friends,
I'll cherish always to the end.

I love the wonderful things you do.
Helping the less fortunate ones than you.
To help them live a better life,
Just as you make me feel so nice.

O yes, we had our ups and downs.
Then you'll sing those lovely songs
And hope will rise afresh once more
Our friendship stronger than before.

These words I share with you today.
Come from my heart like when I pray.
God bless you Baby, one more time.
You are my special Valentine.

THE PENNY ON THE ECONOMY

"I don't believe that they want to talk with me
They think that I'm only a nonentity
But I've been watching the Economy
And I do not like the trends that I see.

"So tell the leaders to come talk with me.
I'm sure I can solve this economy.
It's best to learn from a wise penny.
Than to make life hard for everybody."

"I'm sometimes called a Pretty Penny
So you can really take it from me.
The last thing for this Economy.
Is to apply restricted plastic surgery."

"People are losing jobs almost everywhere.
The markets tell us that things are severe!
I know what's better than the wealthy tax cut
I'll make the economy wake right-up!"

"I know about the events of 9/11
And the global fight with terrorism.
But we have problems right here at home!
Some cannot pay for their telephone."

I want to see people start working again
Adding wealth to the country; not being a drain
And the working class will start jumping up.
When you see all kind of businesses waking up.

"So tell the leaders to come talk with me.
If they want to solve this economy.
It's best to learn from a wise penny
And transform this faltering economy"

WATSON, THE COMPUTER

FEBRUARY 17, 2011

There's a new sensation on the Jeopardy Show
With an IBM computer you probably know.
It competes with two humans for Jeopardy cash.
And its answers were making the biggest splash;

The computer is given the name of Watson.
And there's nothing it seemed to have forgotten
yet it said that Toronto was an American city.
How it arrived at that answer, it really beats me.

One of the two humans playing was Brad Ratter.
The guy with the highest jeopardy earnings ever.
Watson went after them from the very start
As a computer, it knew they were very smart.

In two days ken amassed twenty four thousand dollars
Small, to Watson's pile looking like two twin towers.
Seventy seven thousand, Watson registered on the board.
Not even one third, ken Jennings was able to afford.

Watson had advantages over his human counterparts
Whether the Bible, Science, or the liberal Arts.
He was quick on the buzzer and ready to go.
To entertain the mass audience of the jeopardy Show.

It was a marvel in artificial intelligence
Over the human mind's quest for excellence
It was truly a triumph of the artificial brain,
And we will keep challenging Watson again and again.

THE WORLD'S GREATEST MOM

By Augustine Joseph
International Poet of Merit Award

O How I love My Mother!
And Esteem her high With Praise,
My Mind Delights With Thoughts of Her
This Thankful Child She Raised.

It Takes a Special Lady,
With Abiding Love to Spare,
She Embraced Me From a Baby,
No One Else Like Her Compare!

What Wise and Trusted Counselor!
Advisor, Teacher and Guide,
When I'm Low, She Lifts Me higher,
Always standing By My Side.

O How I Love My Mother!
All My Words Strongly Attest,
For I Searched The World All Over
And Found Out MOM is The Best!

A TRIBUTE

DEDICATED TO:
ST. JOSEPH'S CHURCH, FAYETTEVILLE, NORTH CAROLINA U.S.A
ST. PAUL'S ORANGEBURG, SOUTH CAROLINA U.S.A
ST. JUDE'S CHURCH, BARBADOS, W.I
ST. MARTIN'S CHURCH, BARBADOS, W.I
HOLY CROSS CHURCH, BARBADOS, W.I
ST. CHRISTOPHER'S PARISH, TRINIDAD, W.I
ST. AGNES PARISH, TRINIDAD, W.I.
ST. PAUL'S SANFERNANDO, TRINIDAD, W.I
ST. DAVID'S TOCO, TRINIDAD. W.I

If I were a writer, I would describe each one of you;
And tell all those dear readers the wonderful things you do.

And if I were an artist, I would draw a portrait of each
And use you as examples, in the lessons that I teach.

And if I were a singer, I would sing out to the whole world;
And tell all those within my voice, you're better than all the gold.

And if I were a runner, I would sprint from East to West,
And tell those also North and South, these churches are the best.

And if I were a mountain climber, I would ascend the highest peak,
And shout to all the world below, that you love to look and seek.

And if I were a philosopher, I would pen wise sayings of each;
And use you in my messages, and sermons that I preach.

And if I were a sculpture, I would chisel each one in stone,
And all who pass to see you, would want to be your clone.

And if I were a pilot, I would fly from city to city,
And tell the people living there, about your ministry.

And if I were a monarch, you would be my royal guests;
I'll bid you sign the royal book, reserved only for the best.

And if I were an angel, I would fly to heaven's gate;
And tell St. Peter and all the saints these churches here are great.

And If I were poetic, as I am being now,
I would say: "Hail to all these Churches."
Each one deserves a bow.

BROTHERHOOD

By Augustine Joseph

HOW would you define brotherhood?
For God gave it to us for good!
It is a bond, stronger than steel,
That only those with love can feel;

We need, to deeply consider,
The meaning of the name, Philadelphia,
God sent His Spirit like a dove,
To touch our hearts with brotherly love;

But O what sad story to tell,
When Cain jealously killed Abel;
His brother loved, and ran from strife,
But Cain with envy took his life.

And we can hear that bitter cry,
When Esau, tricked, felt he could die.
Stripped of his birthright by Jacob,
Oh the anguish felt, when he was robbed.

Again, jealousy raised its head,
Where love should be displayed instead!
The Prodigal son, who came back home,
His elder brother picked a bone.

God grant us all to live as one,
Like Moses, and brother, Aaron,
And all the world, will strive for Peace,
As sibling rivalry decrease;

"Brotherhood" is in great demand,
The kind that loves beyond the Klan,
Then we would have true brotherhood,
And God would say, "O Yes, It's Good."

DALE EARNHARDT: THE INTIMIDATOR

What astronauts accomplished high up into space,
Dale Earnhardt, did here on earth.
Unequalied, he was, in the NASCAR race,
He rose to heights, though of humble birth.

His favorite car, decked with the number "3",
And was special with black and silver schemes,
It was fast, and would go to the highest degree,
Dale's mind stayed fixed upon his dreams.

The Winston Cup, he won seven times,
Was indeed a hint of the news headlines,
The number "seven" really means completion,
There wasn't any need for an addition.

Being NASCAR's daunting intimidator,
He was racing around the familiar track,
And as the best know legend of NASCAR,
Dale launched ahead of the angling pack.

But it was on a fateful February day,
On the 18th day of the month,
Thousands of NASCAR's fans would pray,
A tragedy occurred here in the South.

The Daytona 500 Race was apace,
And Dale Earnhardt was the favorite to win,
But his car slammed into a wall and laid waste,
After hitting first, Sterling Marlin.

At the competitive age of just forty nine,
A great champion he was, and won seven.
His fans lamented as he was in his prime;
But was racing instead towards heaven.

The NASCAR legend, Dale Earnhardt,
Leaves memories behind so dear.
He is gone, but his legacy will never depart.
He is accident-free, on the track up there.

MEMORIAL DAY

MAY 29, 2000

The young and vigorous lad was he,
Signed up to defend his country.
His hopes were high; he had no dread.
No fear of death came to his head.

And so he went to Vietnam
To fight the Vietcong in their land.
He fought hard for the U.S.A.,
But fate made claim to him that day.

Others like him put up a fight.
In different wars, the cause was right.
Crimean, Korean, or World War II,
Some didn't make the battle through.

But those who fought but missed the hilt
Should never have survivors' guilt.
If all were victims of the fray,
Who'd live to fight another day?

So on the last Monday in May,
Commemorate Memorial Day.
Remember those who fought so well,
The servicemen and women who fell.

AIR FORCE

The men and women who love to fly,
High up into the awesome sky,
They never fear; their lives at risk,
Could end up fast on a dead list;

They'll fly their planes in rough terrain,
To foil the enemy's plans for fame,
And interrupt their plan attack,
Destroy them, so they won't come back;

The men and women of the Air Force,
With training, skill, they steer the course,
With eagle eyes, the target seek,
Lay it in ruins at their feet.

They'll take their flight to a distant land,
To give others a helping hand,
Their mission is their enemy,
Return to base and family.

Sometimes a life or more is lost,
In fierce attack, or when storm-tossed,
They do it all for freedom sake;
Would fight again; just give the date;

The nation sure has gratitude,
For those who fly high altitude,
To bring down those, like the Titan,
And protect forever, Freedom Land."

VETERANS OF FOREIGN WARS

From time to time, conflicts do arise.
But it doesn't, to any soldier, come as a surprise.
For they pledge to take the fight where they're sent.
If it means living in fox-holes to avoid bombardment.

They leave their home-land, and their beloved shores,
These fearless Veterans of Foreign Wars.
At times, the land was unknown where they did arrive.
But thanks be to God, many did survive.

Of their experiences, some prefer not to speak.
For the battles they fought, were not for the weak.
These sterling Veterans of Foreign Wars,
Believe they always fight, for a worthy cause.

These heroes left behind their worried families,
With their hopes and fears, and anxieties.
They thought of them often, in groups or alone,
Hoping that their loved-ones, safely come back home.

But the unfortunate ones didn't make it back,
Including Vietnam, Afghanistan and Iraq.
They gave their all, the supreme sacrifice,
And for freedom, they did pay the ultimate price.

Their strategy for victory was exceptional.
Fighting in the front line, or as an admiral,
Each time, their life, they did put on the line,
For freedom and all free-loving humankind.

With courage they undertook their high-risked mission,
To bring the enemy into humble sub-mission.
These heroic veterans of Foreign Wars,
Deserve from our nation, resounding applause.

THE GREAT DEBATE

By Augustine Joseph
(Poet of Merit International Society of Poets)

On August 7th in Washington,
A scientific 'war' was head-on.
It wasn't a nuclear bomb at stake,
Yet big enough to seal our fate.
A group of scientists said they've seen,
The need for cloning human beings,
Another group with words, O how strong!
Claimed that their 'friends,' were deadly wrong."
"Research", they say, is premature,
More facts required; keep closed the door,
Rearing to clone someone in haste,
Could implicate the entire human race
They say, . . ." It's merely a matter of time,
Before we clone our humankind
We know enough to have it done,
Despite complaints, we think they're wrong."
The opposing side strongly objects,
To treat people as mere subjects,
"Dolly, the sheep, you longed to clone,
But please leave human beings alone"
"We, on the side of cloning still,
Are itching, eager, to fulfill,
And prove our new technology,
Outstrips all held theology."
"Such arrogance, you I must tell,
Points at the Tower of Babel,
Unstoppable, they think they are,

Insist that they must go that far."
They want to prove, without a doubt
They have the knowledge, power and clout
"Whatever it takes to show they're great,
This act could really seal our fate."
Human beings aren't things or mere objects,
To try to dehumanize, or experiment with.
But some think they have a clear mandate.
So there is no point now, to vacillate.

DON'T GIVE UP YOUR SEAT

By Augustine Joseph

It is a lesson we must learn,
We need the insight to discern,
Despite the challenges we meet,
Don't let injustice take your seat.

Some people when put to the test,
Like Moses in the wilderness,
If only this great lesson teach,
Don't think of giving up your seat.

Rosa Parks taught each one of us,
When rudely accosted on the bus,
Don't ever go down in defeat,
She held her ground, and kept her seat!

You youngsters when you go to school,
Stay there and learn 'knowledge' is kool,
When you're tempted to retreat,
Don't you ever, give up your seat.

You may not like the lesson-plan,
Or Teacher Joe that's in command,
Don't think of rushing to your feet,
Start thinking, hold on to your seat.

If you're convinced that you're right,
And it means that you'd have to fight,
Remember, you must be discreet,
But don't you surrender your seat.

Jesus invited to their home,
Martha got busy on her own,
But Mary sat at Jesus' feet,
Martha couldn't get her from her seat.

Nelson Mandella couldn't reconcile
His imprisonment on Robben Isle
And while in prison, he didn't give up his seat
Until Apartheid's historic defeat.

So I urge you in your country,
Your seat holds opportunity,
Despite the challenges you meet,
Don't let injustice take your seat!

THE DEADLY ROLL IN HAITI:

"MAMA DON'T LET ME DIE!"
BY AUGUSTINE JOSEPH, POET OF MERIT AWARD

1-31-2010

About four in the evening, things began to unfold,
A seismologist, a short while, before had foretold,
"An earthquake is coming, it's due anytime!
'Believe me,' he said, "I see ominous signs."

On December 12, Two Thousand and Nine,
The land was in place, the weather was fine,
But on January 12, Two Thousand and Ten,
Port-au-Prince, was thrown into a deadly mayhem.

Like a crocodile, launching its deadly roll,
Thirty seconds it took, to amass the death toll;
If earthquakes, like hurricanes, were attributed names,
I would certainly name it, nothing but "Insane."

The first rumble, spelled trouble for the state of Haiti,
What a horrific misfortune and catastrophe!
The once stable land began to sway to and fro,
The people confused, didn't know where to go.

In seconds, huge buildings were swallowed up whole,
Like a ravenous monster, it was callous and cold;
People scampered in streets, both the young and the old,
While it continued its rampage, and stranglehold;

People running for safety, were startled and stunned,
Not knowing where to go, their minds bungled and numbled,
While escaping, some ran into danger's way,
Like in the Book of "Lamentations," they cried out that day.

Newsflashes came over the air without fail,
Saying it was 7.2 on the richter scale,
The quake had just raised the poor state of Haiti,
Both the "rich" and poor leveled in poverty.

Countries tried to help, from all over the world,
The destruction was more than what was first told,
Rescue teams set to work clearing heavy debris,
They needed the help of the Lord God Almighty.

America, was one of the first to respond,
President Obama, reached out, above and beyond,
He dispatched the U.S Comfort, the hospital ship,
As well as other personnel fully equipped;

Doctors went out to help, in awful conditions,
Carrying out surgeries, and difficult amputations,
People bleeding from bruises and all kinds of cuts,
Some were lucky to be saved; others they could not;

Days later, a child was pulled out from beneath the earth,
She had gaping wounds and in a terrible state,
She was rushed to a hospital that very day,
But no help was found there; and was turned away!

"Mama," she cried out, "Please don't let me die."
Her mother looked up, full of tears in her eye,
She continued to hold up her little girl's head,
But in minutes Anika, her daughter was dead.

Elsewhere, someone shouted, "You must dig fast right here!"
"Someone is alive, and is buried down there!"
After hours of digging, a hand pushed through the earth,
And a feeling of joy, once more emboldened their work.

It was impressive to see their strong religious faith,
Shame on the self-righteous! Who did castigate,
But in the midst of despair, they gave praise to the Lord,
In life or in death, Jesus Christ is their Lord.

More knocking was heard; and the digging was fast,
Not knowing that the victims were nearing their last,
The rescuers shouted, "Hold on don't give up!"
But then there was silence, the knocking had stopped.

An number of kids, were badly hurt by the quake,
Some parents and guardians met a gruesome fate,
Some children suffered serious injuries,
And many with life-long disabilities!

True, most people will give from all walks of life,
And come to the aid of the Haitians' plight,
Remember the orphans and defenseless children,
If not helped, would be left abandoned, and forsaken;

The Haitians will thank you for all that you do,
They know that you care, and they love you too,
The Lord will say: "Haiti, come forth it is time!"
And the Haitians will rise from the dust, looking fine.

Xxxxxxxxxxx

[[same page already typed BROTHERHOOD]]

"EGYPTIAN REVOLUTION 2011"

It started on the 25th day of January.
A bid to stop the maladies in their country.
Thousands of youths headed to Tahrir Square.
To voice their complaint without timidation or fear.

Two weeks passed by without a resolution.
And the people insisted on his abdication.
But President Murbarak wanted to compromise.
Hoping the situation would soon stabilize.

But most of the people had a deepen mistrust.
If he decided to stay on, there would be utter disgust!
All that they want, is for him to go.
But he was stubborn and resistant like King Pharaoh.

Mubarak said, he holds a Ph-D in obstinacy.
But he never named the school that award the degree!
But I have a conviction with some certainty.
That he got it from King Pharaoh's University!

Mubarak pledged publically to the Egyptian Nation.
That he wouldn't run again, nor seek re-election.
And the U.S didn't want him to leave right away.
For fear lawlessness becoming, the order of the day.

Meanwhile, the Vice-president reach out to the Muslim Brotherhood.
And other important groups to make the situation good.
He offered sweeping concessions including a free press;
Remove the emergency laws which the people detest!

Mubarak tapped into his bag of diplomacy.
But they remembered his Words of obstinacy
That he had a degree in sheer stubbornness.
And his ploy was an effort to overcome this!

Once the protestors' momentum appeared to wane.
To lose such momentum, would be hard to regain.
But they kept pouring into Tahrir Square.
And it became evident Mubarak didn't have a prayer.

They became braver, and bolder up to the palace gate.
And Mubarak watched the crowds as they congregate.
Rumors said, he was going to address the nation.
To bring the whole crisis, to a resolution.

He felt staying on till September, was better for him.
But the people didn't want to hear, any such thing!
There was one point they wanted, him clearly to know,
The sooner, the better, he had to go!

Some felt the Vice-president would be leader instead.
But some didn't see him as a replacement head.
Some said, he also belonged to the Mubarak regime.
So he is guilty and dirty as Mubarak has been.

It was Lord Acton of Britain who had this to say.
It rings true, for the whole world, up to this day.
He said, "absolute power corrupts absolutely"
It took 30 brutal years, for Mubarak to see.

An official pronouncement came from the palace.
That, President Mubarak, was about to give place.
He was vacating the presidency once and for all.
He felt it was time for him to make the call.

It was February 11, the pronouncement was made.
And the people start jumping like a happy parade.
The country would be left in the best of commands.
The military will prove the most competent hands.

The people teary-eyed, and excited with joy.
Watched the leadership fall like the City of Troy.
But no weapons were drawn; no gunshots were heard.
Anywhere near the people amassed in the road.

Over 300 people gave their lives for the cause.
Fighting for human rights and a land of just laws.
The blood that was spilled, was not spilled in vain.
If they had to do it, they'd do it again.

It took 18 days, for Mubarak to step down.
This was the hope of the people in protest all along.
They laughed and they cried with many tears of joy.
For they knew it was real, and no longer a ploy.

ABILITY

MAY, 2000

"I have no skills at all," you say,
A thing you've heard 'most every day—
And so you've come to hold the view
That there's nothing you can do.

Others tell you, "You have no skills!
The good Lord gives to whom He wills,
And you must stay within your range.
Your life will never, ever change."

Dismiss this twisted view of life.
Such negatives are very rife.
Remember, those who fail to try
Will never reach where eagles fly.

You have great wealth that's deep within—
The power to act, release your wings.
Start working now to venture out.
Never, ever, feed on your doubt.

Your gifts are there, though covered up.
Begin to dig, and find the spot.
You'll prove them wrong and smile in glee.
Show them you have ability!

BARBARO

A race horse of promise came fast on the scene.
To some the young stallion was inept and green.
But yet he was ready and eager to go.
His name was the unheard of Barbaro.

Millions that day watched the race on TV.
The annual event, the Kentucky Derby.
The stallion raced forward and galloped up front.
And decided to stay there until the last count.

Crowds on their feet as the race heated up.
And Barbaro sensed victory of the Derby Cup.
The action was tense, you could see it on each face,
That Barbaro had the lead and had won the race.

The fans couldn't wait, to see him race again,
They wanted to witness his second rise to fame,
But minutes into that big decisive race,
Barbaro made a lurch; and he couldn't keep up the pace.

Lamentations were heard from almost every point,
Barbaro's right hind leg, slipped out of joint.
Million disappointed, shouted, "Barbaro!
Oh Barbaro, Oh Bar-ba—ro!"

XXXX

POLITICAL POLEMIC

AUGUST 2, 2000

Whenever comes election time,
Each party claims, "This time is mind!"—
Argues the ruling party failed;
"A lot more people should be jailed."

"The others said they failed to see.
Look at the strong economy!
We know how much you'll love to show
That many more deserve Death Row!"

"Hold it, you liberal-in-thought!
Don't take away the guns we bought.
The people closely taking note
Are sure to give us all their votes."

"How sad if this were really true."
You wish that power'd come to you.
The surplus is your money tree,
To spend it like a lottery."

"The money is the people's own.
They should have it, all alone.
So give them now a tax relief.
(Keep it, and make yourself a thief!)"

"Good try, my friends—Republicans.
Remember, aged Americans,
The day is coming fast, you see.
Where is Social Security?"

"We'd rather concentrate on schools.
Right now we have too many fools.
They have to learn to pass the test,
And our party does it best."

"But who increased the working class?
Reduced the homeless very fast?
It's our party, we Democrats.
That's why we will be voted back."

And so each party's point of view
Is targeted to you and me.
At last the voters have their say:
They give it on Election Day.

All racial groupings, live happily in Trinidad,
And we de-emphasize the racial card.
By our watch-word is stated: "Every creed and race."
In Trinidad and Tobago, "finds and equal place."

THE CONCORDE

The year was 1969

It was manufactured in both French and British design.
And aircraft that previously, was only a dream,
Came for the first time on the European scen.

It looked like a craft just from outer space,
It was fast and would win in any aircraft race.
Majestic and artistic in its poise and stance,
In flight it will only afford you a glance!

The Concorde created for those who were rich,
And want to arrive at their destination quick.
When lesser folks like us, won't be able to afford
The rich, with ease, were flying on the Concorde.

Thirty years in flight without a single flaw.
The Concorde traversed high over sea and shore.
With awesome and impressive supersonic speed,
High up the affluent love to read.

Then the year 2000, July 25th appeared.
On a flight to England, no one really feared.
The Concorde's records no one could deprive,
Was about to end in a sudden nose-dive.

An oblong-shaped fire raged brightly in the sky.
On-looker knew that many passengers would die.
Over 100 lives on the Concorde were sadly lost
But we can never really tell the true human cost.

So the plane that was unrivalled for a very long while,
Transporting the wealthy and others in style,
Came sadly to an abrupt, and sudden end fast,
Now the rich must return to other airlines, first class.

BLOODY SUNDAY

By Augustine Joseph

John Lewis said he'll never forget,
That day in Selma, they came close to death,
When troopers ready, all dressed up in blue,
Attacked them mercilessly without a cue.

Injustice, they couldn't stand any more,
Each day they saw one more racial flaw
So Blacks went out to protest in peace,
But Selma troopers attacked brutally and wouldn't cease.

Arriving at the Edmund Pettus Bridge,
Scenes gruesome, made world-wide coverage,
An order was given for them to disperse,
But sooner than later they'd be facing the worse.

The troopers came armed with weapons and sticks,
And clubbed the marchers with dreaded bull whips,
Some struck in the head, blood flowed all around,
While trampling horses kept them on the ground;

"If we are denied our rights here at home,
Should we seek it outside this Freedom Zone?
No! We make just claims in this land of our birth,
Our forefathers' blood also drained in this earth."

The scenes on that Bridge was too graphic to see,
But it helped all the marchers win great sympathy,
"How can any leader in Freedom Country,
Allowed such oppression; inhumanity!

The Alabama cause reached the President's ear,
And President Johnson denounced the affair,
In a televised speech called it "deadly wrong"
Referring to the song, "We Shall Overcome."

One week later, their needs were addressed,
The Voting Rights Act was on the President's desk,
He quickly signed it and made it the law,
That voting encumbrances must be no more!

But John Lewis, and others are still on the 'march',
To remind this great nation of its solemn task,
For a nation that preys on its own folks at home,
Will weaken forever, its own backbone.

CLEAR SKIES

By Augustine Joseph
(Poet of Merit Award)

I'm checking all of the fifty States.
For good weather above the rest,
Dark clouds and I just can't relate . . .
Clear skies are what I like best.

In Mississippi and Alabama,
And the Carolinas as well,
Rains torrent into a mighty swell,
Newsmen have so much to tell.

Georgia's no different from Florida,
From where Hurricane Andrew came,
And in Arkansas and Louisiana,
Strong winds can drive you insane.

The Central States, like in Nebraska,
Live the Killer Tornado Winds,
And in New Mexico and Arizona,
The sun's deadly like scorpions' stings.

I'm checking each of the fifty states,
For the weather that meets the test,
Dark clouds and I just can't relate,
Clear skies are what I like best

From New York across to Washington State,
Are fine, if you like the cold,
But I'm telling you the chill won't abate,
Young people even look old.

Hope seemed to lie in the Golden State,
Live there, you really can't fail,
But who can forget that mighty Quake,
Nine point five on the richter scale.

I'm checking each of the fifty states,
For the weather that meets the test,
Dark clouds and I just can't relate,
Clear skies are what I like best.

MYSTERY DOG

A smart dog, I'll call him Rover.
Had a wonderful life in Wichita.
He had lots of space, by no means a small room
His owner always had him very well groomed.
One day he did something that was very strange,
He walked away like someone going insane!
No arguments at all, not a word of strife
Rover randomly left and walked out of their life.

The owners cried, "Rover, please come back home,
Life out there is too hard being alone,
Tears in my eyes as we worked the telephones,
We beg you dear Rover, please come back home."

Even in the month of November, 2003
They didn't give up still hoping to see,
Their dog they wondered where could he be?
They knocked on every door, hoping to find the right key!
But one day, they couldn't ask for anything more:
A dog came by sniffing outside their door.
They looked and thought it was all a dream
Awe—struck by what they had really seen.

"Rover, oh Rover, you came back home.
Life was too hard out there being all alone
Six years have passed since you went out to roam.
Thank God, dear Rover, you came back home."

XXXX

THE FELINE-CANINE RIVALRY

The dog, once number one in the home,
Somehow, seems to have lost its bone.
The cat has taken now its place.
At home we see a whiskered face.

Cats wear a very pensive look,
As though they read us like a book.
They have an independent will.
Call them: they remain standing still.

A dog will wag its tail and come.
Fast to its master, quickly run.
But not a cat: it's wild, it's tame,
It does not always play our game.

Cats carry some superstitious tale,
It matters not, female or male.
If on a tombstone you see a cat,
The devil they say, has that soul intact.

A cat can climb the tallest tree—
In danger, seek security.
Its paws give traction right up to the top.
But it can't get down as it was going up.

The cat is pet to rich and poor.
You'll find it home at any door.
But though it's loved a little more,
The dog wants the place, it had before.

THE WHISTLE OF DEATH

AUGUSTINE JOSEPH

Shirlely Bassy sang it, "The Kiss of Death"
A fate that awaited the young Emmett,
The Chicago youth, just 14 years old,
Caught up in a racial stranglehold!

It was in August, 1955,
Emmett Louis Till was full of drive,
He visited friends in Mississippi,
And was overwhelmed by racial savagery;

The horror offended some kind-hearted whites,
Who joined in the fight for Civil Rights,
"Emmett, whistled at a white woman,"
And enraged some members of the Ku Klux Klan!

Abducted and shot in the barbaric style,
He was dragged by the neck for a long, long while,
His body, they dumped in the Tallahatchie,
His face was so marred, ask his mother Mamie.

Two men apprehended for the hateful crime,
"They'd pay by death, or they'd do the time!"
But a prejudicial and all white jury,
Came back with the verdict: "Not Guilty!"

This blatant injustice, blacks fuming to see,
Among them, his mother, Mamie Mobley,
She died, still while grieving, with a heavy heart,
But Keith Beauchamp pledged to work on her behalf.

And so with some clever detective work,
Beauchamp start digging till the main line broke,
More evidence surfaced, and started to flow,
"Back to the courthouse, this case must go!"

And so Emmett Till, will take one more step,
In search of justice, for his "Whistle of Death;"
And hope that the jury selected this time;
Will make those responsible pay for the crime!

MONTYEL POETRY CONTEST
SUBMISSION 9-30-2000

THE SILENT KILLER
BY AUGUSTINE JOSEPH

It stalks its victims, quiet, straight,
It's full of patience as it waits,
Intends to harm and slowly kill,
Destroys its prey, yet living still.

It's present whether day or night,
As victims for their lives they fight,
A husband helpless, hopes his wife,
One day sees her gets back her life.

The nervous system under attack,
Stealth-like advances, won't turn back,
It's time we fight back hard and strong,
Until the victory is won.

We can't permit this killer loose,
To prowl the land as with a noose,
To take the life of any one,
Yet go unchallenged town by town.

We need a prayer; a treatment soon,
To render help before high noon;
Multiple Sclerosis is its name,
It's time we kill it; end the game.

Written by Augustine Joseph
837 Durwood Drive,
Fayetteville, NC 28311

THE ABC'S OF MOTHERS

AUGUSTINE JOSEPH

A—Mothers are like angels: they're always watching over you.

B—Mothers are like Bibles: they impart godly wisdom each day.

C—Mothers are like cookbooks: they give instructional recipes for life.

D—Mothers are like doctors: they'll work on your heart if they have to.

E—Mothers are like engineers: they'll make a way to your goals in life.

F—Mothers are like feet: they'll show you the different walks of life.

G—Mothers are like generals: they'll go to war to protect you.

H—Mothers are like hospitals: no wonder you call them Doctor Mom.

I—Mothers are like injections: sometimes the hurt is for your good.

J—Mothers are like Jesus: salvation is their main concern.

K—Mothers are like knowledge: they hold the key to your future.

L—Mothers are like lighthouses: they'll warn you of the pitfalls of life.

M—Mothers are like Mary: they ponder over the meaning of their kids.

N—Mothers are like newspapers: they always have news for you.

O—Mothers are like an orchestra: they'll help you attain a standing ovation.

P—Mothers are like prayers: they talk to God on your behalf.

Q—Mothers are like questions: they'll help you find an answer even if you
Think you already have one.

R—Mothers are like radios: they want to know whom you're listening to.

S—Mothers are like statesmen: they rock the cradle and stabilize the world.

T—Mothers are like telephones: they're always available to talk.

U—Mothers are like universities: they'll go to any degree for your success.

V—Mothers are like vice-presidents: they're very important people.

W—Mothers are like writers: they can produce volumes on your life story.

X—Mothers are like Xerox: there is much you can copy from them.

Y—Mothers are like yearbooks: they always have memories of you.

Z—Mothers are like zeros: they're indispensable to your life, as Y2K is

to the new

Millennium.

THE ABC'S OF FATHERS

By Augustine Joseph
(Poet of Merit Award International Society of Poets)

A—Fathers are like Airports; they provide the means for kids to launch out in life.

B—Fathers are like Benefactors: they give quality time to their kids.

C—Fathers are like Calculators: they can figure out their contribution.

D—Fathers are like Dictionaries: precise: they get to the point in a word.

E—Fathers are like Exercise: it takes training to meet all responsibilities.

F—Fathers are like Firemen: they'll rush to your rescue day or night.

G—Fathers—are like Generals: they plan strategy for your success.

H—Fathers are like Hotels: they always make room for their kids.

I—Fathers are like Institutions: they must handle every case at home wisely.

K—Fathers are like Kings: They teach their kids the refinements of life.

L—Fathers are like Land: they prepare the foundation for building lives.

M—Fathers are like Mentors: they give the best advice to their kids.

N—Fathers are like Nationalities: they teach their kids to respect all people

O—Fathers are like Oxygen: they are life-giving forces in their kids' lives

P—Fathers are like Professors: they are teachers in the university of life

Q—Fathers are like a Quorum: they must accept decision-making.

R—Fathers are like Religions: God is a reality in their lives.

S—Fathers are like Stars: they provide shining examples to look up to.

T—Fathers are like Tires: they perform best with the right pressure

U—Fathers are like the U.S.A: they are of many shapes and different states.

V—Fathers are like Valedictorians: they speak glowingly of their kids.

W—Fathers are like the White House: they do more than occupy space;

They are admired by every race

X—Fathers are like X-rays: their kids see through them for better or worst.

Y—Fathers are like years: some become wiser with the passage of time.

Z—Fathers are like Zones: some seek comfort; others love a challenge.

BLACK HISTORY MONTH

FEBRUARY 17, 2001

A people rich in mind and thought,
Like others, once were sold and bought.
Though body held in prison, bound,
The mind, unchained, sang freedom song.

Necessity commanded them,
To tap their imagination.
Slavery kept each one all alone;
Slaving away at the grinding stone.

Blacks were great inventors, you should know,
Creations of Black minds aglow.
The view that Blacks aren't very bright,
Is a plan to keep them from the spotlight.

The kids of today must quickly discern
That their future is knowing to learn and earn.
And that the hardest workers in the ignoble past,
Want us to exceed any given task.

Black History teaches prudence and fortitude
Courage we must muster with gratitude,
Gwendolyn Brooks and Rosa Parks.
Did insist on us scoring higher marks.

Think too of Woodson, Mays, and King,
And yes, Clara Brown and Richard Allen.
Also sweet-scented Madame Walker's Cream
Help to keep alive Black people's dream.

Black History wants the youths to know
That life today was not always so.
For some, freedom was just only a hope.
Their lives ended, without casting a vote.

Yes, deprivation is very much with us still.
They withhold the technology that would enhance their skill,
They gave them tests, but just for the show.
Then they describe them as lazy and slow.

Black History helps us all to reflect
The evil past and its bad effect
But now the future is open; somewhat wide.
We have to be ready to step inside.

O obstacles, each day still abound,
Incarceration is seen all around.
To some this land is far from free
Justice for Blacks is no guarantee.

But Black History's Month cannot really contain,
The vast achievements Blacks still attain
But it helps us pledge to work all anew.
To mountain-climb, but not just for the view.

STOP THE BULLY

There's a serious problem now in our schools,
A few lawless kids won't obey the rules,
Every child should be free from abuse, you'll agree,
And not be controlled by any bully!
Bullies are emerging all over the place;
Some are even located in cyberspace!
Kids hate going to school, because of what they know;
The taunting from the bully they have to undergo!
Bullies instill great fear in the ones they target,
Take even their school lunches, and eat all of it!
Their goal and their purpose is to greatly offend;
And do as they please, it doesn't matter when.
The victims are hurt to the point of tears;
And in silence they think that nobody cares!
Some say nothing, and let the thugs have their way;
While the poor kids are going through hell every day!
Some kids contemplate acts of suicide,
For from the bully they know that they cannot hide.
If the kid does not fit in he is ridiculed as sick,
And on him they'll always harassed and pick.
Tell the bully that our kids have had enough!
We must resist in ways that are effective and tough,
If the bullies think they can do as they please,
They will meet community action that's hard to appease.
So tell the bullies they are not welcomed here!
Call in law enforcement, and it's a different affair.
Everyone must expose and stop the bully
No more silence and fear; no more secrecy!

A MUSICAL TALENTED PEOPLE

Two islands in the open Caribbean Sea,
Were politically married in harmony,
In 1899 the union came forth,
Since then, they never entered a divorce court.

A people talented and culturally rich
Could tune a steel pan to the highest pitch.
With composers, calysonians as well,
All masters of their music just like Handel

Names like Beethoven, Tchaikovsky and Mozart
Joseph Haydn, Chopin and Sebastian Bach,
We have composers too, that you'd one day know
I'm sure you have heard of the Mighty Sparrow

We love our soccer, netball and cricket
You should hear the crowds with an English wicket!
But the part of the culture that grabs us the most,
Is the carnival celebration from coast to coast.

Designers like George Bailey, Ken Morris and Peter Minshall,
Add great creativity to our carnival,
Bands like Despers, Hatters, and Trinidad All Stars
Play pan music so sweet, prisoners break out of their bars!

The streets come ablaze in colors all bright.
In the Caribbean sun, O what a delight!
People "chip" to the music and masquerade all day.
And on Ash Wednesday they go to Church to pray.

Trinidad has a rich oil-based economy,
Trinees travel year-round, the whole world to see,
If you go to the North Pole a Trinee is there.
One was talking to Mars asking, "What is the Fare?"

Trinees love their delicious crab and calaloo.
And the Indian dishes like doubles and spicy curry,
Who could forget the mouth-watering chicken roti
And our traditional African style cookoo.

All racial groupings live happily in Trinidad,
And we de-emphasize the racial card.
By our watch-word is stated: "Every creed and race."
In Trinidad and Tobago, "finds and equal place."

THE OSCAR SCRIPT

The night of the Oscar, is about to take place.
It's an extravaganza, with many a smiling face.
It is a night that the nominees, couldn't wait for!
Everyone in their finest, you couldn't ignore.

The red carpet is laid and is quality rich,
Like royalty does it, always dressed to enrich;
The nominees and guests all "dressed up to kill"
In cool or warm weather, or a nipping chill!

Each nominee, brings something in particular,
It's a very important piece of paper,
It's the script with some winning words, unknown to us!
We'll hear them when the lucky name is called out thus:

". . . . And the Oscar goes to . . . . we will soon hear it,
The winner pulls out the script and reads in a high pitch.
But we are left speculating, what other actors did write!
We won't know, as they didn't walk the red carpet that night.

LETTERS

Letters are just like people,
With different moods and swings,
In their message they are able
To tell us several things.

Sometimes they're very bitter
Sometimes they're very sweet
Sometimes they're just for the litter
To place on the garbage heap.

And there are those we'll always cherish
And kept preserved a whole lifetime,
We make sure they never perish.
Their thoughts are most sublime.

And there are letters historically old,
That St. Paul wrote with love
They speak directly to the soul.
Inspired from God above.

But in one way letters do differ.
From us human beings at best.
They are obedient ever
To the thoughts we want expressed.

They tell us too the state of mind,
The high points and the low.
The words we write will master-mind.
Which place our letters go.

XXXX

EXTRAORDINARY MEN
(By Augustine Joseph)

Father's Day 2010

Men of different levels in stature and height;
See the work of a father their greatest delight;
With love for their family; at least, most of them!
I suppose that's because they're extraordinary men.

There's an incredible passion as they go out to earn,
Within them, their heart intensely burn.
For they know as breadwinners mouths depend upon them;
I suppose that's because they're extraordinary men!

They teach their kids, to know the rough terrains of life,
To live and let live; ignore useless strife;
Seek to avoid the enemy, but make another good friend,
Good advice, as they are extraordinary men.

They take note how society has changed over the years,
And has brought on anxieties and rational fears!
So they impart wise teachings, others do comprehend;
Because they are just that ! Extraordinary men!

Kids use names of endearment, like "daddy" and "pop";
But if found doing wrong, they'll demand that they stop!
For good dads will insist on what's right to the end;
Because they are mentors, and extraordinary men!

So on this auspicious occasion of Father's DAY,
We thank God for them as we sincerely pray;
That those who could do better, and choose to amend;
Will enhance their role more, as extraordinary men!

Xxxxxxxxxxxxx

DANCING IN THE MORUARY

It happened in the dead of night,
It was a weird and eerie sight,
To see him dressed up all in black,
He almost gave me a heart attack.

The sound of music was uncanny,
Coming from a nearby mortuary,
Curiosity got the better of me,
So I went in search for the cause to see.

I peeped once and twice in great disbelief,
And started to shake like a helpless leaf;
For what I saw peering through a hole,
Was too diabolic a thing to behold!

The light was dim, yet I could clearly see,
This drama unfolding right before me,
Mortician White, held a piece of cord, in his glee
And started to dance alone in the mortuary

He waltz through the spaces with a one-two-three,
The words that he sang seemed to make him happy,
"The best thing," he said, "that brings joy to me,
Is seeing my morgue filled to capacity."

The music was customized just for the dead,
With choreography he touched each corpse's head,
And from one's ear pulled out something like wool,
And sang out in joy, "Yes my mortuary it is full."

WISHFUL THINKING

If I were a lawyer,
Profit wouldn't be my aim;
But defense of all my clients
Whether dirt poor or of fame.

If I were a politician,
Power wouldn't be my goal,
But to fight for truth and justice
For the least ones in this world.

And if I were blessed with riches,
Luxury won't be my style;
But to help the ones who struggle
With finances all the time.

If I were an orator,
I would speak out loud and clear,
With eloquence and wisdom
Till my message reach each ear.

And if I were blessed poetic
I would write and write each day;
Till all the world read line by line
What poets do have to say.

If I were a great investor
Affluence, I would not seek
But invest in people's power
Help each one stand on his feet.

THE MIRROR'S MESSAGE

MAY, 2000

We visit it each morning
And often times each day,
And just before reclining,
To bed after we pray.

We won't avoid the mirror.
It has a lot to say.
It points us to each error
Before we go our way.

Some things can't be corrected,
No matter how we try.
The mirror's job, completed,
Reveals what missed the eye.

Someone was disappointed.
With wrinkles on her face,
She smashed the glass to pieces
For telling her the case.

We can't predict the message
The mirror has to say,
But those who are delighted,
Longer they view and stay.

THE PENDING SUIT

NOVEMBER 29, 2000

I've always had a lovely name
I'll cherish evermore.
The Presidential election came:
Now I'm not very sure!

For on the day that I was born,
My parents called me Chad;
But now my name is full of scorn.
I wish they never had.

I never doubted I'm a dad.
I know I never will.
The Electors called me Pregnant Chad.
This is a bitter pill!

No crime deserving death I've done.
Nor had my day in court.
But I was dubbed The Hanging Chad.
Condemned! I should've fought.

Destruction of my name persists.
The networks, frenzied, grab.
An explanation—I insist!—
For calling me Punctured Chad!

The Supreme Court must hear my case,
Restore my hope in Chad.
I want that smile back on my face:
The good name that I had.

REVELATIONS IN SPACE

I looked up one day at the open sky
And asked the questions, "who?" and "why?"
For I was truly seeing the hand of God,
The Almighty One, He is the great Lord.

The clouds I beheld were like wool from heaven
They scurry along as with haste wind—driven
Some cirrus thick clouds sailed steadily above,
At a glance they appeared like a flock of white doves.

Sometimes the clouds did seem to cooperate.
And formed images on which to meditate.
An artist couldn't get a better scene to draw,
Their "landscapes" breath-taking, left me filled with awe.

Above them, you could see the skies all blue
The works of the creator was shining through.
The awesome vastness was itself a sign
I was in fact beholding God's amazing design.

We see the sun descending low in the west,
It is obedient to the Lord God Almighty's request.
"So you're amazed and wonder about my retreat
You must know the one that gives me my heat!"

The astronauts who soar high up into space,
Have seen God's mysteries face to face,
They know that science cannot really compete,
With God enthroned firmly upon His great seat.

XXXX

THE TEXAS SEVEN DECEMBER 2000

This news we all will remember,
Made headlines in late December,
That seven men broke loose from prison,
They call the group, "The Texas Seven."

Their crimes, though many, one was top,
It was for killing a Texas cop.
Armed with weapons of lethal kind,
A big reward to boost the find.

The seven, ruthless to the core,
They had no respect for the law,
Lawmen were warned to make no stop,
Until the seven were all locked up.

Six weeks had passed without a lead,
Fearful citizens took more heed,
Some felt they went to Mexico,
But others doubted it was so.

Then one day at a trailer park,
The police tipped with a head start,
The convicts went to Bible class,
Displayed God's love there very fast,

The police came and stalked the house,
And one was trapped there like a mouse,
Instead of giving up his fight,
A shot rang out, he took his life.

Four of them nabbed without a fight,
Security tightened left and right,
This took place in Colorado,
A fair distance from Mexico.

But two still remained on the loose
Had quickly sought to make a truce,
Surrendered, taken back to prison,
Last chapter of the Texas Seven.

MY MOTHER'S NAME

Some people seek power, fortune and fame,
And others climb heights of mountains' terrain
But all I do wish, in sunshine or rain,
Is hearing the sound of my sweet mother's name.

And still there are others that would travel afar.
In outerspace to see a bright morning star.
But one thing I seek over and over again.
Is hearing the sound of my sweet mother's name.

And there are those who seek power and authority,
To be in absolute control of their land and country,
But thanks be to God, He is all my gain
And allows me to hear my sweet mother's name.

There are those who like digging for silver and gold.
In search of fine jewels in part of this world,
But I still hold firmly, and would say it again,
I love to hear my sweet mother's name.

Yes mother dear, I do cherish you.
There isn't a price tag for the things you do,
Your loving care is my sweet refrain.
God bless you Mom, in his holy name.

XXXX

THE NIGHT BEFORE CHRISTMAS

It was a sacred and holy night to see,
What God had planned for you and me.
God's Son preparing to come to us.
The night of hope before Christmas.

Mary and Joseph was in search of a place,
The mother to be, was full of grace.
But no place was found for them to stay.
So both of them began, in earnest to pray.

Angels above were about to sing,
To herald the Child that would be the King.
Shepherds that night, kept watch over their sheep,
Would see sheer amazement at their feet.

It was the night before the Day of Christmas,
The Lord was coming to save all of us,
Peace and good will to all human kind,
He would open the eyes of all who were blind.

Wise men will bring their symbolic gifts'
From now on, each one heavy burden lifts.
The angel told them what his name will be,
"Jesus," the Savior, for everybody.

The word made flesh will dwell among us,
Such thoughts of joy before Christmas,
That's why I invite you to come and sing;
Glory to God, our newborn King!

XXXX

SNAKES

They always held deep dread and fear.
In ancient Egypt, they were there.
In ancient Rome and Bible times
The snake's menacing look you'll find.

They lurk in walk ways, sand and grass,
Ready to strike you, when you pass.
With flickering tongue and lethal fangs.
Excruciating were those pangs.

Among the dreaded ones we know
The carpet viper's poison flow.
No provocation for it strike.
Pass by, you'll get that fatal bite.

Some view these creatures as evil.
Incarnate of the real devil.
Egyptians held a different view
The Cobra brings immortality.

The heaviest snake, it loves the water.
Is South America's Anaconda.
It weighs well over a thousand pounds.
The Water helps it to move along.

The longest fascinating snake,
Its appetite large to compensate.
The reticulated great Python
Wraps all its victims all around.

It loves monkeys and jungle cats.
Guards all its eggs till they are hatched.
Pythons can spend some nineteen months
Without tasting even an ounce!

Scientists say that long ago,
All snakes had legs to make them go.
The Python! What a constrictor!
Inhabits the Southeastern Asia.

The snake has an intimidating look,
Be careful walking near that brook.
And in case you may have forgotten
It caused Adam and Eve to leave Eden.

THE KEYLESS SOCIETY

I wonder who is the inventor of the key?
Something that gives us security!
Like Alexander Graham Bell's great telephone
The key provides safety to our home.

What would life be without a key?
We leave our house behind, but with anxiety
We go to our work, but our minds think of thieves
Rummaging in our drawers with consummate ease.

Tell me what would life be, without a key?
Our car in the parking lot for all to see,
There it is parked, without any lock:
It could be vandalized right there on the spot

You might be wondering, how did the car arrive here?
When there was no key for you to drive it there,
This highlights the complexity without the key.
For it makes life more difficult for you and me.

What would life be without the use of a key?
How would banks secure the people's money?
Anyone can go freely to see what they find.
Prisoners would be free to roam anytime.

What's the point of a locker then at your school?
Anyone can flip it open without a tool
IF kids have access to everyone's things,
They'll make sure they take all of your belongings.

What would life be without the use of a key?
You might have a visitor you didn't want to see!
At nights when you think you're safely in bed.
You could find a stranger standing next to your head.

ENDEAVOUR'S LAST MISSION

May 16, 2011

(1) Her husband carried her wedding ring into space:
And by looking at it, he would see her face,
She also kept his, as a reminder on earth,
Of their exchange of vows made as strong as girth.

(2) Giffords joined five other astronauts families,
To view the lift off observed with some anxieties,
From the commanding view, of Kennedy Space Center,
They viewed the rocket-propelling, rearing Endeavour.

(3) It was Endeavour's last voyage, taken for Uncle Sam,
After an adventurous, and historic 30 year old program
But its imminent withdrawal brought tears here at home,
Including an Italian crew member, who'll return to Rome.

(4) And after a successful lift off, hugs were all around.
From the thousands gathered to see the launch from the ground.
And while Endeavour disappeared quickly out of sight,
It brought the space program, once more into the spotlight.

(5) The Flight, originally scheduled for April 29th,
But no endeavor, is ever sealed, watertight.
And at the 11th hour, emerged and electrical problem,
That required a suspension and a postmortem.

(6) When Giffords saw it was a successful liftoff,
She was heard to be saying: "Good stuff, good stuff."
It was headed to the International Space Station,
To leave a magnetic instrument for cosmic information.

(7) Gifford's wore her husband's ring round her neck, on a chain,
     Her love for Commander Kelly, will forever remain
     And even though a gunman pierced the left side of her brain,
     We are hopeful she will recover to serve her people again.

(8) It was Endeavour's secret plan for a launch suspension.
     For on that date, Prince William married Kate Middleton.
     But Endeavour wanted to have the whole world's attention
     As it was leaving on its last historic space mission.

(9) So Endeavour had a day devoted solely to itself,
     No distraction from it's high position on the shelf;
     And blasted off flawlessly, at the count—down to zero.
     And with rocket speed, through the clouds it did go.

XXXX

POWER BLUNDER

A legend told us of a King;
Who wanted wealth from everything.
His name was Midas.

The story says, he made a wish,
To have fulfilled things on his list;
He got his heart's desire.

He longed to have the Midas' Touch,
To change anything on the spot;
And that was what he got.

Intoxicated with such power,
His ambition rose like a Tower;
And still he wanted more!

And so the legend, we are told,
The King wished for everything gold,
His eyes could not behold!

So one day seated at a meal,
His appetite, he couldn't conceal;
The table richly spread.

But O, alas! It came to pass,
The King was thirsty; took his glass,
It turned into gold fast.

He tried again to get some food,
Gold bars appeared; inflamed his mood,
How sad to see him brood!

He pleaded to reverse his state,
But things were final and too late;
What thoughtless, mindless fate!

Leaders today, still act this way,
Make rules in haste; we left to pay;
Like Midas in his day.

SCHOOL BUS BLUES

I love all of our school children,
And the pursuit of their education,
I love each parent and guardian
Who see them through to their graduation

But the thing that upsets me the most
Is the sight of that yellow bus,
That signals to stop right in front of you
Especially when you're in a rush.

I love the educational slogan
That says: "No child left behind!"
I love how devoted the teachers
Who are caring, loving and kind.

But the thing that I dread the most,
Is the sight of that yellow bus.
That stops abruptly in front of you,
Especially when you're in a rush

I love their counseling program
That fights all illegal drugs,
And condemning the other bad choices,
Like being bullies, unruly and thugs.

But the thing that I hate the most,
Is the sight of the yellow bus
That seems to drop anchor in front of you
Especially if you're in a rush!

COOL RED HAT DAMES

You'd think royalty runs in their veins,
The distinguished and elegant Red Hat Dames,
Their stately poise pleasing to behold,
Women in red hats story must be told.

The idea came to Sue Ellen Cooper,
Who visited a thrift store as a buyer;
. . ."I'm going to buy something else," she said.
But soon that red fedora was on her head.

Her mind profusely thinking of bigger things,
Her racing thoughts seemed to acquire wings,
"Women, can be whatever they want to be;
If I form a Red Hat Society:"

So women start forming groups almost everywhere.
To shop, and dine, and their lives to share,
Doing acts of kindness, but not for fame,
The gals known locally, as the "Cool Red Hat Dames;"

Those under fifty decked themselves in pink hat
With lavender dresses, they all attract,
But regardless of the color, whether pink or red.
These women's groups, suddenly began to spread.

They mix with folks out of every state,
Helping women to step out in faith,
Women who lost the spark, in their life they once had,
Reclaimed it and now they are very glad.

"Don't think that your life is over the hill,
You have great inspiration in you still,
Join us and you'll see that it is true,
What the Red Hat Society will do for you!"

AIR TRAFFIC CONTROLLERS

They are the airlines traffic lights,
That control all the airplane flights,
They speak with pilots in the air,
And tell them when landing is clear.

They speak with pilots on the ground,
About to take their planes along,
Prepare them on the runway strip,
Before they take off on their trip;

'Air Traffic' is a work of skill,
It's more than just an act of will,
It takes training like works of art,
To keep those zooming jets apart.

Their work is often over-looked,
We think more of the flight we booked,
But were it not the 'Tower Guys'
There would be horrors in the skies.

THE DINOSAUR

By Augustine Joseph

Millions of years in that wild atmosphere,
Lived the prehistoric creature, the dinosaur,
Some twelve species of varying size,
Fought to be victor, or become the prize.

The Tyrannosaurus proved awesomely fierce,
With claw-like feet its victims pierced,
Its name bears the meaning, "Tyrant Lizard King,"
Others thought twice, before challenging him.

A mouthful of sixty, ready sharp teeth,
Coupled with strength and some vicious feet,
It grew to great length, over fifty feet long,
Its arms, though were short, were very strong.

Some ripped away flesh like the true carnivore,
Others preferred plants, like the known herbivore,
But regardless the choice of their menu each day,
If you came upon one; talk to God, don't delay.

Dinosaur's once roamed all over the world,
From Argentina to Utah their story is told,
In Egypt and Germany, England and France,
Their fossils were found by design and by chance.

Like turtles, the dinosaur also laid eggs,
Unusual for creatures with four sturdy legs,
Paleontologists also found remains in Spain,
I wish these reptilians were living again.

"THAT'S MY DAD"

If you heard of a man who understands,
And in good and bad times, still holds your hand.
That is my Dad.

If you know of a man who stands with you;
No matter the problem your going through.
That is my Dad.

If you heard of a man, as a great mentor,
And shows you opportunities through life's corridor,
That is my Dad.

If you heard of a man, who is an inspiration;
And shows you the importance of a good education.
That is my Dad.

If you know of a man, who really cares,
And knows the importance of daily prayers;
That is my Dad.

And if you know of a man, who knows his Father;
Jesus Christ our Redeemer, Lord and Saviour;
Believe me, that is my Dad.

THE CELL PHONE CRAZE

What a wonderful achievement! What a welcomed device!
But it's interruptively noise, like the telemarketers' vice.
Some deem it a milestone in man's invention,
Others dislike its frequent interruption.

But while people are airing and sharing their views,
The cell phone keeps ringing even in church pews.

The cell phone craze is seen everywhere,
When praising the Lord, the cell phone is there.
You enter a room posted up, "Silence please!"
The cell phone is loud, you just won't believe.

I saw a man walking down a busy street,
Ear glued to his cell phone, while he was on the beat
A driver came by, nearly hit the man,
A cell phone too was in the driver's hand.

The cell phone craze is seen everywhere,
At a funeral service, or the hour of prayer.
I often wonder, where it will be heard next.
Maybe in a casket giving out its last text.

But you should be careful of the cell phone's use.
It's important to guard against its abuse.
Avoid holding the cell phone too close to your ear,
Indiscriminate use, could bring on a nightmare.

The cell phone use is rapidly on the increase.
Experts say, close contact with the ear must cease.
The warning goes out, "you could be in danger,"
Overtime it could lead to serious brain cancer.

THE QUEEN MARRY II

1. What magnificent gliding on the open sea!
    Our mouths agape by its immensity!
    The Queen Mary II, left Southampton's great shore,
    On April 16th, Two Thousand and Four;
2. Unmatched and unequaled among the ships,
    She crossed the Atlantic, on her inaugural trip.
    She encountered great billows, and in the quiet of dawn,
    Docked in New York City, on a Thursday morn.
3. Gracefully, gliding under the Verazzano Bridge.
    A masterpiece too, O how creative!
    With security tight, yes, more than ever!
    She routed royally up the Hudson River.
4. Onlookers amazed by the close-up view;
    Saw its 3,800 passengers and crew.
    Its awesome size made the Titanic look small
    Twenty one storey high, tell me that isn't tall.
5. Her length was an impressive eleven hundred feet,
    One billion in cost; what a magnanimous feat!
    She glanced at the Concorde, now a museum piece,
    Her day too will come; from all duties release.
6. But now is her time of luxury in the sun;
    A two-storey theatre and a planetarium;
    An exquisite Art Disco completed the scene.
    This "palace" on water, befits a great queen.
7. A ship of this stature propels into fame.
    Especially one designated with the Queen Mary's name!
    The wealthy cannot wait to go sailing abroad.
    They will meet her in spirit; she is somewhere aboard.

Xxxxxxx

CAYSEA ANTHONY-JURY-FURY

1. A young mother was charged with killing her baby,
   Her name was given as Caysea Anthony.
   The case was intriguing, and gained interest world-wide,
   Everyone wanted to know, how little Caylee died.
2. Every day of the trial, there was a rush to get in,
   The first ones arrived there, early in the morning.
   The lucky ones got a ticket, serving as a passport;
   That would give them access to a seat in the court.
3. The court scenes were in Orlando, Florida.
   Where the Prosecution and Defense battled each other!
   Both teams skillfully displayed, good theatrical might,
   The news media described it a gladiatorial fight.
4. How the 2-year old died, no one saying at all,
   Grandparents still in the dark, after making their call!
   Those who knew, were not talking or telling the truth,
   Getting to the facts, was like looking through soot.
5. Caylee, the only daughter, of Caysea Anthony,
   Was missing 31 days, and kept in secrecy,
   Her remains were found later, in a swamp among trees,
   And Law-Enforcement, swooped down, like aroused hives of
   bees.
6. After such a long time, the body will decompose,
   How the body got there, no one really knows,
   There was duct tape around the child's mouth and nose,
   Who really put it there? Only God alone knows!
7. The police questioned Caysea, to get at the truth,
   But she guarded her lies, like a robber his loot!
   She told them different stories, that didn't add up,
   So they insisted and told her the lies must stop.
8. The defense argued that Caysea learned to lie from home,
   It wasn't a trait she developed, all on her own,
   Therefore, she couldn't be held wholly responsible,
   For some things she had said, about missing Caylee.

9. She told them she was working at Universal Studio,
   When they asked for some facts, she really didn't know,
   It soon became clear, that it was all a big lie,
   And Universal Studio, was her pie in the sky.

10. She was arrested, and brought to court to be tried,
    To answer the charge as to how Caylee died!
    The case then had become a world-wide sensation,
    People followed it closely on their television.

11. A tattoo, at a back shoulder, says "A Beautiful Life."
    But Caylee wouldn't grow up, to be someone's dear wife!
    Only Caysea can say how her daughter died,
    But she preferred in the court, just to whimper and cried.

12. They discussed funeral rites of passed pets in the home.
    But no rites for Caylee, just dumped and disowned!
    The people were angry, and offended by this,
    And their clamorous cry was for Caylee's justice!

13. Caysea, was depicted as the partying mom.
    Who would frequent the night clubs to have lots of fun!
    The Prosecution contended, Caylee was in the way,
    And restrict Caysea's freedom, and games she would play.

14. No report about Caylee for 31 days!
    After such a long time, evidence could erase,
    The child's decomposed body was eventually found,
    Not far from their home in a bag on the ground.

15. The prosecution contended, Caysea killed her daughter,
    And should be found guilty, of pre-meditated murder!
    She would destroy anything that obstructed her goal,
    That led her to commit a crime, callous and cold!

16. It's believed she gave Caylee, some chloroform first.
    To make sure, that things didn't turn out for the worst.
    Then duct tape was applied, across the mouth and nose,
    And put her in the car trunk, a thing she alone knows.

17. But on returning, she saw Caylee, with no signs of life,
    So she thought up, a story-line as sharp as a knife.
    Speculation was rife and all over the place!
    When you give people the blanks, they'll fill in the space.

18. The Defense argued that Caylee accidently drown.
    In the family swimming pool, where she slipped and went
    down!

Caysea panicked and hid the real truth of the death,
Because of sexual abuse and its traumatic effects!

19. Yet they did seek the help, of a search volunteer team,
But if the child was drowned, where else she could be seen?
"We spent thousands of dollars searching everywhere.
But it was a waste of our time and grossly unfair!"

20. The defense, accused her father of sexual abuse,
Saying, that that was responsible for Caysea's acting obtuse.
Not reporting about Caylee for 31 days,
"Was disturbing," they said, "but it was only a phase!"

21. A sexual abuse charge, is always tough to hear.
Whether true or false, it is mentioned out there.
And the jury as they sat, and listened to the case,
Would have lingering thoughts, "Did it really take place?"!

22. The trial lasted as long as a month and a half;
The country seemed in mourning, but the flag wasn't half-staff
It took some eleven hours, for the jury's verdict;
And when it was announced, the people didn't like it.

23. She was declared free; of crimes against Caylee,
And the people were in an uproar with the jury.
"Had they considered the facts in its entirety,
They would have come with a verdict, in favor of Caylee."

24. Lightening struck a tree, where the remains were found,
It left many bewildered, and profoundly astound!
Like Moses' revelation, of the "Burning Bush;"
God was making a statement again for justice.

25. Some juries, by nature, are very complex,
They make some strange decisions, that leave us perplex.
All juries should be able to think on their seat,
Like one jury I read of, that is hard to beat.

26. A murder-accused, knew that he couldn't get away,
But his Defense told a story to see how it would play!
He pointed, and told the court to "look at that door;
Because the real murderer will walk through it for sure;"

27. Everyone was fixated on the particular door;
Expecting to learn something, they didn't know before.
But the lawyer told the court, it was something he made up,
And he's going to prove something "right here on the spot."

28. He said although it was a story, he had just thought about,
    His intention is to prove "an element of doubt."
    "The fact," he said, "everyone did look at the door,
    Was proof, they won't certain of his client's guilt for sure!"

29. He told the jury, to consider what he had just said,
    "And acquit his client to go free instead.
    For this is what the case is really all about,
    An unmistakable revelation of an element of doubt;"

30. The jury went to deliberate, with much to think about.
    Especially, the strong argument of the element of doubt;
    But it took just one hour, to get a sound verdict,
    They concluded the accused man, was guilty of it.

31. The judge asked the foreman, if they decided the case?
    He said "yes" and looked straight at the accused man's face.
    "We the jury," he said, "found the accused man guilty.
    And we did so with absolute certainty!"

32. "The Defense," he said, "argued with eloquence and more,
    And implored the whole court to look at the door;
    Everyone did comply; only one did not look,
    And that one is your client, clearly on the hook."

33. "We had no other choice," said the insightful foreman,
    But to reach no other verdict, than the one in hand;"
    Oh, how I wished Caysea's jury was probing, as this one.
    No question at all; justice would have been done!

Xxxxxxxxxxxxxxxxxxx

FATAL ATTRACTION

I am amazed by what I see,
When others live carelessly free,
They take the path to death so soon,
Fatal attraction seals their doom.

I see it in the highway speed,
A driver fast; abandons heed,
He would not brake; his mind is set,
As though he had a date with death;

I see it in the drugs they take,
The pushers know that it's a bate,
The "fish" incline to take a look,
Before you know it, they are hooked.

I see it in some youths today,
Behave as thought they will not pay,
Ignore the counsel of the wise,
And soon regret what they despise.

I see it on the Internet,
Where millions log on to the set,
Unhealthy menus some are fed,
Like flies entangled in the Web.

It's there in the racial divide,
Poisonous hate, some do not hide,
"A house divided cannot stand;"
Christ said it: some don't understand.

What explanation here present?
Is fatal attraction the intent?
I'm puzzled by this path of gloom,
Embrace death faster, than a zoom.

LABOR DAY

(1)   It bears a name that you might think,
For you're given here no hint,
It's clear to me, what these words say:
"You have to work on Labor Day!"

(2)   But Labor Day is free from work!
No working person drives a stroke,
It's a day from work; don't see the place;
No chance to see the boss' face.

(3)   New Yorkers flee the working street,
Seek places of leisure; friends to meet.
No thoughts of work on Labor Day.
Go anywhere, for hours and stay.

(4)   September marks the last quarter of the year.
A time to show the workers that we care.
They do much more than earn their pay.
That's why they celebrate today!

XXXX

GOAL-SEARCH

1. People world-wide have different goals to meet,
   In opposite directions they look and seek.
   From early dawn, till throughout the night,
   Their goal is the main thing they have in sight.

2. Look, how many people are traveling east!
   They feel that their chances of hope will increase;
   Their dream is a goal-oriented intent,
   To achieve all of their goals accomplishment,

3. I see others headed, with a westward speed,
   "Go west" they say, "to implant the seed."
   They too, have their personal goals ahead,
   That will one day earn them their daily bread.

4. Others prefer to join the northern flow,
   The north has more opportunities than others know,
   They're excited and eager to say, "Goodbye to the south."
   In pursuit of employment for a hungry mouth;

5. Yet there are those who nostalgically, speak of the south,
   They know what being there is all about,
   For them, it is neither, east, west or north
   Yet, one may find someone there good to betroth.

6. Yes, some do go east, and some do go west,
   In different directions, they seek out their quest.
   Some go to the north, and some south proceed,
   Their aim is mainly to earn and succeed.

7. So know in which direction, lies the best hope,
   Avoid all the places that love the tight rope!
   You might hear a voice saying to you, "Go north my friend!"
   Who knows? This could bring your goal-search to an end.

Xxxxx

THINKING BIG

THINKING YOUR WAY TO SUCCESS
By Augustine Joseph

The mind is one of our greatest gifts,   Folio No. P2102873
When we are down, it can give us a lift,
We can accomplish our goal by applying the mind,
Engage it, and put it to use every time.

Thinking can make most things possible!
Positive thoughts tell you, "You are able!"
O yes, there'll be others, who just will not see,
How you can make dreams a reality

A philosopher said, "I think, therefore I exist"
His mind told him of things he just couldn't resist!
He chased all his doubting thoughts far away,
And said; "I am real! I am thinking each day."

Question yourself to find answers untried,
Think "outside the box"; feel your thoughts like a tide,
Bathing your mind with new ideas to try,
Ask the root questions, how? When?, Where? And why?

Think big always; don't ever think small,
Something Jesus encouraged his disciples all.
They accomplished so much, with the mind as their link,
That's why Jesus often asked them, "What do you think?"

If you don't change your thinking, you won't make progress.
Or else you'll be sure of the same or regress,
Make it your plan, to succeed in your goal;
And thinking will put you on top of this world.

DAD WAS BORN A GENIUS

By Augustine Joseph
(International Society of Poets)

Dad you were born a genius!
You always knew what's to be done
Your love of home and all of us,
Brought you delight and fun.
Dad you were born a genius!
You kept us tidy and neat,
You kept us safe while on the bus,
We seldom walked the street.

Dad you were born a genius!
You sent us daily to school,
We learned about Pythagoras,
You gave us the vital tools.
Dad you were born a genius!
Church was the place to be.
To grow up without knowing God,
Was like a non-swimmer out at sea.

Dad, you were born a genius,
Hunger kept far from our door,
We learned about Profit and Loss,
And a thousand others more;
Dad you were born a genius!
You taught us the love of books,
You told us they're far better;
Than our facial looks!

Dad you were born a genius!
Our lives are richer because of you,
WE cherish those things with value,
And all because of you.
Dad, you were born a genius!

THE SUCCESS FLAME

By Augustine Joseph

I went to school eager to learn,
So in the future I could earn,
But obstacles in class remain,
But I kept trying over again,

Called up one day before the class,
The verbs I used were green as grass,
I felt embarrassed and couldn't explain
But I kept trying over again.

When later I applied for work,
Employers meant to keep me broke.
The Lord said, "Call upon my Name,"
So I kept striving hard again;

I took classes in writing skills,
To be accomplished like George Wills,
"The next world, maybe, you'll have fame,"
But I kept trying over again.

Within me was a great desire,
Burning intensely, like a fire,
No one could ever quench that flame,
So I kept trying over again.

Now I can read and write and spell,
They marvel how I've done so well,
Ignore those doubters and their game,
Each time they doubt, I rise again.

MUSIC

A beat a song, a chant a tune
Is never early or too soon.
The rhythm speaks to someone's soul,
No matter whether young or old.

Each culture has its song and beat
That move the people off their feet.
They exercise with grace—or prance.
(They can't resist the call to dance!)

Each beat is special to the ear.
The dancers show you what they hear—
A rhythm that's too good to pass.
Slow-moving or pulsating fast.

It may be country, jazz, reggae . . .
Someone is deeply touched that way.
Music does really speak to all;
Just watch them move in the dance hall.

It may be classic, calypso,
Percussion, drums, some lyrics slow.
They follow where they hear the beat
That says, "You must give up your seat!"

The pace may change to one of praise.
In worship, see their hands upraised.
They shout and sing and clap their hands.
The rhythm tells each one to stand.

But there are times when, slowly sung
(You sit in prayer, head lowly hung),
The music makes you contemplate
What love can do to those who hate.

Music, indeed the food of love,
Resides with God in heaven above.
We know too well the angels sing.
"Hosanna to our Savior King."

SNIPER ON THE LOOSE

1. Their peace had been snatched from them overnight.
   A sniper was shooting anyone in sight.
   With telescopic lenses, and a high-powered rifle,
   He had all in the community totally unravel,

2. His victims unaware of being in danger's way,
   Might not have had a prayer before their doomsday!
   The marksman took aim, none to interrupt,
   And the victims fell down, writhing on the spot.

3. He then vanished away in the wooded unknown,
   Leaving those not yet dead, with a helpless moan
   The Washington DC folks, and those in Maryland,
   Would have welcomed anyone with a helping hand!

4. The normalcy of walking was normal no more.
   You couldn't take kids to school or go in a store
   You couldn't go to a gas station or fill up at the pump;
   You couldn't escape the gunman, even if you could jump!

5. An air of uneasiness was over the whole land.
   Both children and adults could not understand.
   Why anyone would disrupt their lives so completely,
   Leaving so much distress and uncertainty!

6. Yes, thanks to law enforcement, for always taking care.
   But for divine intervention, the people turned to prayer.
   Yet they wondered and pondered, some deeply perplexed!
   Each one asked with foreboding: "would I be next?"

BRAINCELLS OF LOVE

I went to the library to read a book
So I sat at a table to take a look.
I didn't expect what I was about to hear,
For the very short time I was sitting there

A boy and girl were at a table nearby,
He looked at her with love in his eye
Then he began to speak to her tenderly
And he said to her very passionately:

"If you want to know how much I love you
Well each of my braincells thinks of you.
In my waking hours and when I sleep
I can't describe it, my love's too deep!"

I tried my uttermost to concentrate,
But he drew closer as if to illustrate,
He said, "Lilly dear, what a lovely name!"
And then he whispered once more to her again.

"If you want to know how much I love you,
Each of my braincells thinks of you.
In my waking hours and when I sleep,
I can't explain it, my love's too deep."

GRANDMA HIT SONG

I still wonder sometimes, if my grandma is dead.
While sleeping, she woke me one night and said;
  "My grandson, please ask anything of me,
  And I will try to make you very happy."

I said, "Grandma I want to write a lovely song,
  To play on the radio all day long,
  I want it to have a sweet melody.
To have the folks dancing well over eighty!"

She said, "Write about the Patriot Act,
  It's controversial, I know, and that's a fact.
But tell them this land must always be free,
  For we cherish our priceless liberty."

I said, "Grandma, this song needs a rhythmic beat,
  To sweep everybody off their feet
  I want the lyrics very east to sing.
  Fit for a commoner; fit for a King!"

The music must pulsate deep in their souls
  In summer weather or winter cold.
Grandma I know that you have the recipe
  That's why you decide to come to me."

She said, "Write about the Economy
It's the engine that drives any size country . . . .

And write about the constitution
The bedrock of this great and inspired nation.
People come from all over the world to be here.
To fulfill their dreams that they cannot elsewhere."

She said, "They love this great country, and free atmosphere,
And no place better suited, to fulfill their career.
She said, "Speaking to you son, was very nice
But I have to leave you now, so just take my advice."

THE POTHOLE

1. It wasn't too big and it wasn't too small.
   And no one paid attention to the danger at all.
   Vehicles drove by swerving left and right;
   Avoiding the pothole, both day and night!

2. So the pothole was a threat, to all motorists.
   If I were to describe it, I would call it high-risk.
   Any unsuspecting motorist or absent-minded driver,
   Could put oneself into serious danger!

3. But no one stopped to look or to mend the pothole.
   Each one was saying that it wasn't his role.
   So day after day the pothole there remain,
   And the hole became wider, and it wasn't the same.

4. But a busy grandmother was thrown into a fit!
   In haste her left front wheel went deep into it!
   The impact was loud; the jolt was severe.
   She went through the windshield; almost lost her life there.

5. So here's a lesson that will always ring true,
   Never put off anything that you know you can do,
   Fill up any pothole that's needed to be filled,
   You might prevent your own best friend from being killed.

INTRODUCTION TO MY FATHER

My Father is

An Aspiration
A Blessing
A Champion
A Decision-Maker
An Encouragement
A Family man
A Guidepost
A Handbook
AnInspiration
A Joy
A Keystone
A Listener
A Master
A Necessity
An Out-going Dad
A Peace-Maker
A Qaulity Individual
A Reflection
A Seeker
A Teacher
An Umbrella
A Visionary
A Well-Wisher
An Xtraordinary man
A You-are-always-there-guy
A Zealous Soul